Lighthouse People

Stories of Men, Women and Children
Who Worked and Lived on Lightstations
in
Newfoundland and Labrador

Jim Wellman

Lighthouse People
Stories of Men, Women and Children
Who Worked and Lived on Lightstations
in
Newfoundland and Labrador

ByJim Wellman

CREATIVE PUBLISHERS
St. John's, Newfoundland
1999

© Jim Wellman

Le Conseil des Arts | The Canada Council
du Canada | for the Arts

We acknowledge the support of The Canada Council for the Arts for our publishing program.

We acknowledge the financial support of the Government of Canada through the Book Publishing Industry Development Program (BPDIP) for our publishing activities.

The poem, "Erosion" (page 14), is taken from *Complete Poems/E.J. Pratt*; edited by Sandra Djwa and R.G. Moyles, University of Toronto Press, ©1989, and is reprinted by permission of the publisher.

Cover Art: Les Noseworthy

∞ Printed on acid-free paper

Published by
CREATIVE BOOK PUBLISHING
a division of 10366 Newfoundland Limited
a Robinson-Blackmore Printing & Publishing associated company
P.O. Box 8660, St. John's, Newfoundland A1B 3T7
First priting November 1999
Second printing June 2000

Printed in Canada by:
ROBINSON-BLACKMORE PRINTING & PUBLISHING

Canadian Cataloguing in Publication Data

Wellman, Jim, 1946–

Lighthouse people

ISBN 1-894294-14-9

1. Lighthouse keepers — Newfoundland — Biography.
2. Lighthouse keepers — Newfoundland — History.   I. Title.

VK1027.N5W44   1999   387.1'55'0922718   C99-950223-9

Dedication
For all the Lighthouse People everywhere who so unselfishly dedicated their lives to saving others.

Table of Contents

Introduction

At first glance, their work may look more or less the same as many jobs. Like others, that is, if you don't consider the danger, the harsh environment, the winds that never seem to cease, the isolation, the responsibility, and the loneliness.

Their work is not just a job. Their work is a commitment — a dedication to a service unlike any other.

They are lighthouse keepers.

They are the men and women who, along with their families, have dedicated their lives to saving others from certain death in storms and unforgiving seas.

Since the early nineteenth century, hundreds of those men and women have worked and lived in lighthouses that dot the necklace of headlands surrounding the coastline of Newfoundland and Labrador.

Their job has been to keep the lights burning and the foghorns bellowing to warn marine traffic of impending danger. That's what they've been paid to do. Their actual work has gone far beyond that. There's hardly one of them who has not participated directly in a rescue effort in one way or another. That involvement ranges from alerting rescue authorities of sinking ships to personally pulling shipwrecked victims from the ocean. Some lightkeepers have died trying to save others.

Stories from lighthouse people about tragedy and tragedies averted are endless in every location where lighthouses have been established. Unfortunately there are few records of those incidents, largely because lightkeepers consider it merely part of their everyday work to save a life, hardly giving second thought to it. That would be too much like patting yourself on the back as far as most of them are concerned.

Lighthouse People is not a historical record of lighthouses and their keepers in Newfoundland and Labrador. Rather, it is a collection of some of the stories about a small number of those very courageous and special people.

IRELAND'S ISLAND
painting by Les Noseworthy

Located about three miles offshore from La Poile Bay on the southwest corner of Newfoundland, Ireland's Island is just a rock, barely large enough to support a large building. No one lived on the small island until a steel lighthouse was established there in 1886. In 1891, the population of Ireland's Island was three. According to the 1945 census, the population had tripled to nine people. W. Hickman was the first lightkeeper on the small island. Other early lightkeepers were James Simms and Frank Read. Mr. Read operated the light until 1919 when Henry Chant took over, beginning an association between Ireland's Island and the Chant family that lasted until the 1990s. Assistant lightkeeper Philip Chant was swept overboard and drowned while working on the island in the early 1940s. The last lightkeepers to live there year-round, were brothers Randell and Albert Chant. Their brother, Calvin Chant, maintained the light on a contractual basis for the Coast Guard until 1992 when the light was fully automated.

Chapter One

Coast Guardians

A Different Kind of Life

Lighthouses have become symbols of stability in modern day culture. In a world where hardly anything remains the same for more than a few days, lighthouses continue to be the stoic beacons of light and hope they've always been. Lighthouses don't run around all over the coastline looking for someone to rescue — they just stand there and shine.

Lighthouse people are like that too.

The first lighthouse in Newfoundland was built in St. John's by private enterprise in 1813. Tired of losing cargo and ships that frequently foundered on the rocks trying to find the way through the famous St. John's Narrows, a consortium of Water Street merchants built a lighthouse at Fort Amherst at the south entrance to the harbor. Because the entrance is small and narrow, navigators needed to be "dead on" in their reckoning. Disaster was imminent if they failed to clear the treacherous cliffs of Signal Hill on the starboard side or Amherst Rock/South Head on the port side. The merchants' decision to build a light at Fort Amherst may have been given impetus in the last two years before construction when no less than three ships were lost. On December 4, 1811 a large schooner, *Paradise,* struck North Head across from Amherst. Five passengers, two men, two women and a girl, died. The vessel's cargo of fish and oil was also lost. Less than two weeks later, another schooner, the *Betsy,* out of Nova Scotia, crashed into the cliffs of South Head at the base of Fort Amherst. The Captain and one crewmember were lost. Her cargo of coal and other provisions also went to the bottom of the harbor where she sank in just minutes after striking the cliff. The following summer, the *Vulture*, a large schooner from England, was lost trying to find her way through the entrance to the city.

Those incidents made it imperative to construct some sort of navigational aid to the busy port of St. John's. Since the Governor of the colony had only recently granted people permission to build permanent houses in St. John's, the timing in 1812 was right. The Fort Amherst Light operated from voluntary contributions by St. John's business people until 1835 when it went under the control of a new government board called The Commission of Lighthouses. Within fifty years of the construction of Fort Amherst, dozens of lighthouses and fog alarm systems dotted the coastline of Newfoundland and Labrador, providing beacons of safety and security to the busy marine traffic along the shorelines.

The men and women who worked and lived in lighthouses are a breed apart. While overall working conditions have dramatically changed in the last twenty-five years, some things remain the same. In many ways they still live in a world of their own. Today's lighthouse keepers work at a job that has neither a beginning nor an end to the workday. Even when they're asleep, they are on the job.

Lighthouses look the same; it's the way they are managed and operated that has changed. The lighthouse is no longer a permanent home to anyone. There are no families living on lightstations in Newfoundland and Labrador anymore. These days, lightkeepers work shifts similar to firemen and offshore oil workers, working twenty-eight days on location followed by twenty-eight days off.

By their very concept, lighthouses are almost always remote from the rest of the population. Because they are usually located on high cliffs, totally exposed to nature's most ferocious beatings, lighthouses were not comfortable places to live and raise a family. Those brave men and women who, along with their families, chose to live and work in such an environment are very special people.

Stories of courage, bravery and heroics are commonplace when lightkeepers talk about their peers. Ironically though, lightkeepers seldom view their own acts of bravery as anything more than simply doing their jobs. As often as not, they'll focus on the lighter side of an

Camp Islands — Larador

otherwise tragic story. Instead of the tragedy, they talk about misunderstandings due to language barriers or cultural differences involving foreigners. Other times, their stories are lighthearted reminiscences of crude, albeit effective, measures to nurse shipwrecked victims back to life after narrowly escaping death. But always, the truth is about a class of people who constantly put the lives and the well-being of others ahead of their own comfort and safety.

In the days when lighthouse keepers worked on lightstations for nearly twelve months a year, they lived in a world that, in many cases, was literally all their own. Usually perched on desolate rocky headlands with just their own families, they lived with the best and worst of nature. On a sunny summer day, the view from a lighthouse is breathtaking. Viewing a sunrise or sunset from atop a lighthouse on a clear day is, for some, akin to a spiritual experience — the beauty is simply indescribable. In the fury of a February nor'easter, lighthouses are subjected to the nastiest beatings that nature can deliver.

Weather is a constant source of concern for people on light stations. While strong winds occur almost daily, storms often lash at headlands with ferocity unknown to urban dwellers.

Frank Myrick is still amazed that there was no loss of life in a storm in the early 1960s when winds were clocked at 104 miles per hour on Cape Race. Frank says everything that wasn't bolted down blew off the cape that day. "It was impossible to stand up against the wind," he says.

Max and Faith Sheppard wonder how they managed to escape injury one stormy night when seas constantly crashed over South Head creating foaming white water that flowed all the way to the lighthouse residence door, nearly a hundred feet above sea level. Faith was so worried that the seas might flood her house she bundled her children in warm blankets and took them to the safety of the lighthouse tower situated on higher grounds. Keeping watch on the residence from the tower, Faith stayed there with her children until the next day when seas retreated.

Walter and Betty Strowbridge remember when hurricane force winds ripped the door from the lighthouse residence on St. Jacques Island on several occasions. "It was impossible to hold the door," Walt says. "The best you could hope for was that the winds wouldn't carry you over the cliff with the door. I also remember winds so powerful, railings were ripped off posts."

Fred Osbourne says the roughest weather he can remember was on October 19th, 1976. Stationed at Cape Race at the time, Fred left his home in Trinity Bay on Tuesday morning to start his twenty-eight-day shift at the lighthouse. The weather had become so rough by late morning that Fred had trouble getting across the twelve-mile road from Portugal Cove South to the cape. Heavy seas breaking over the shoreline were washing across the road leaving tree stumps, rocks and other debris in their wake. After finally picking his way through the obstruction, Fred faced another dilemma when he arrived at the lighthouse. The winds were too high to open the front door of the residence. With the help of fellow lightkeeper Noel Myrick, Fred eventually managed to get his supplies into the house through a back entrance on the leeward side of the winds.

Shortly after getting settled, Fred and Noel were startled by a thump against the wall followed by a loud hissing noise. "The thump wasn't a like a hard smack, it was more like thunder rolling," Fred says. Thinking the extreme winds had blown something against the house, the two men were still confused by the strange hissing sound. Looking through the window they soon realized the hissing was the sound of saltwater retreating from the hill in front of the house. The thump was actually the sound of a huge wave that smashed against the cliff, shooting water and spray more than a hundred feet in the air to the top of the cape near the house.

Farther north along the coastline that night, high seas also broke out windows in Memorial University's Marine Science Centre in Logy Bay, near St. John's — the first time seas had reached that level of the building.

That same storm claimed a Dutch cargo vessel southeast of Cape Race. The *Gabriella* succumbed to the vicious winds and seas when her cargo shifted, causing a serious list to the starboard side. The fifteen crewmembers were forced to abandon ship. Thirteen of them perished before their lifeboat was found near Cape Pine.

Tom Ryan remembers a storm that drove seas more than a 150 feet up the cliffs of Belle Isle. Tom is certain the seas reached that height because casks of provisions that were stored at the 150-foot level were swept into the ocean. Tom and his fellow lightkeepers could hardly believe their eyes to discover that mountainous seas had washed all of the oil drums and food supplies from the storage area.

To exist in such harsh environments, lighthouse people honed their survival instincts as sharp as a razor's edge. Resiliency takes on new meaning for people who live year-round on a barren piece of rock in the North Atlantic Ocean. Sometimes the population of the entire community would be less than ten people. If the plumbing rusted or if the generator broke down, there was no hardware store around the corner where they could go and pick up a replacement part. It was up to the lightkeepers to devise a makeshift survival plan until a Coast Guard ship or coastal freighter brought the proper

Courtesy Doug Peet

A typical supply vessel bringing provisions to remote lighthouses in the spring and fall.

replacement part. Usually, that took several weeks. Sometimes it took months.

Nothing Taken for Granted

Routine everyday functions that were taken for granted by most people in Newfoundland and Labrador often presented lighthouse people with their greatest challenges. While most Newfoundlanders have mail delivered either to their doors or to a nearby post office, picking up the mail on Camp Islands in the 1960s was more challenging. For lightkeeper Tom Ryan, mail was always "airmail." Tom's mail was literally dropped from the air. Even parcels were dropped from a fixed wing aircraft that would swoop down to just feet above the rocky island off southern Labrador once every second week.

Mail plane on Belle Isle, equipped with skis, circa 1949.

The plane was the regular mail carrier to communities up and down the Labrador coastline. Usually flying a twin-engine Otter or Beaver aircraft, the pilot would circle the island two or three times to alert Tom and the assistant lightkeeper Lance Bartlett that they had mail. "We'd hear the plane and then we would walk up to the hill and watch and wait as he circled around until finally he'd fly in just over our heads and drop a mail bag out from the cockpit window and we'd catch it," Tom says. "After a while we came to recognize the pilots because they would come down low enough that we could get a good look at them when they'd drop the mail bag," Tom laughs.

Adapting to the lifestyle in a lighthouse environment was not always as easy as developing a creative mail delivery system. Sometimes, providing basic services for a home called for more than

Courtesy Canadian Coast Guard, Fisheries and Oceans

Milking cow — a common daily chore for lightkeeping families.

creative imagination. Malcolm Campbell and his family ran out of water one summer on Gull Island. Located three miles offshore from Cape John on Newfoundland's northeast coast, the island doesn't have a pond to provide a consistent water supply. Because of its haystack shape, there's not enough level land on the small island to support a pond large enough to hold more than a tub of water.

The Coast Guard built a large cistern that remained nearly always full from rainwater funneled to the tank through a system of drain-pipes. But in 1975, the rains didn't come. After a long hot dry spring, Malcolm and the families of the two assistant lightkeepers started rationing their daily water usage in July. But the dry spell continued. By August, the 1000-gallon cistern was empty. "There was hardly enough left to fill a mug for a cup of tea," Malcolm says. Coast Guard authorities dispatched a helicopter to ferry water from La Scie, White Bay, to the island. Using empty rum barrels to transport the water, the helicopter crew worked two days filling the cistern with enough water to last several weeks. Fortunately, the weather returned to normal and within a few days, regular rainfalls supplied the Gull Island cistern once again.

There are times, especially in winter, when it is impossible to get on or off islands in Newfoundland and Labrador. Ice and poor weather prevent helicopters from landing. The absolute isolation means that dealing with death requires creative thinking. A man died on Belle Isle one winter in the 1940s. Because the island was surrounded by ice, it was impossible to get his body off the island to his hometown for burial. The lightkeepers decided that the only way to preserve the body until spring was to use the same method that fishermen employed to preserve fish in summer. Placing the body in a small storage shed, they covered it in salt and ice. Months later, when navigation opened, the body was taken home.

In the days before VHF Radio, lightkeepers on Ireland's Island near LaPoile devised a flagging system to notify people if there was a death. The lightkeeper flew the flag at half-mast until someone, usually from LaPoile, noticed and sent a boat to enquire what had gone wrong.

The Fishermen's Friend

Lighthouse keepers around the coasts of Newfoundland and Labrador had daily contact with inshore/small-boat fishermen. Usually the interactions were by VHF Radio and although they never met face to face, numerous close friendships were fostered through the voice-only contact. Some lightkeepers tell stories about fishermen they communicated with hundreds of times but have never met face-to-face.

Lightkeepers often had access to information that was vital to fishermen. Often that information had to do with weather conditions and forecasts. Other times the lightkeeper might have news about ice conditions in the area. Lightkeepers, especially those on headlands and capes that rose hundreds of feet above sea level, could look down from their lofty lookout point in the light tower and see what ocean conditions were like for miles around. Even today, sealers in the Twillingate area often depend on the lighthouse keeper on Twillingate-Long Point to keep them informed about where seal herds are located. More importantly, sealers want the lightkeeper to keep them up-to-date on rapidly changing ice conditions. Fast-moving ice can lead to disaster if sealers can't see what is happening.

Dozens of sealers on the northeast coast say they would have been stuck in ice for days had they not been alerted to the changing conditions by the lightkeeper. Others claim their small wooden-hulled boats might have been crushed to pieces if they weren't warned by lightkeepers to move quickly when ice floes began to surround them. From the lighthouse the lightkeeper would direct the boats to open water leads, out of harm's way.

Rough arctic ice often moves silently but quickly along the northeast coast of Newfoundland in spring. As it constantly changes configurations, depending on winds, tides and currents, the large ice pans can surround and trap a vessel for weeks. A sealing crew from Conche was trapped in ice for nearly four weeks in the 1980s. Skipper Ben Foley says it was the longest and most boring four weeks of his life. Unable to do anything but wait for the ice to loosen, the crew stayed onboard to ensure the boat was not crushed by rafting ice pans. The only thing the crew could do was walk across the ice floes to nearby Grey Islands for a stroll every day. "It was a tough spring that year," Ben says.

Like fishermen and sealers, lightkeepers easily adapt to the inevitable mood swings of nature. "You got to take the bad with the good," they all say. Taking the bad includes accepting the fact that they can't always get home after their twenty-eight day shift has finished. High winds and seas can halt vessel traffic to and from islands for days on end. After nearly a month working on an island, lightkeepers are understandably anxious to get home but patience is often a required virtue. It's not unusual to have to wait three or fours days to get off an island. Lightkeeper Eric Kendell from Fortune wrote a song about being stranded on Baccalieu Island after completing his shift. Although he was accustomed to being island-bound, this time was different. It was just a few days before Christmas and he was particularly anxious to get home for the holiday season. Besides that, he was

Courtesy Canadian Coast Guard, Fisheries and Oceans

Unidentified lightkeepers and their families — probably on Sunday outing about 1900, apparently not very excited about having picture taken.

suffering from gout. The lyrics of the song sum up the terrible disappointment of being held captive on the island but the last verse illustrates the typical acceptance of "the way it is" when you're a lighthouse keeper. He called the song Layaway.

Layaway
I'm just an old lightkeeper boys
On this station doing my job
I'm stuck here on this island
And this time, I think I'm lost
And the wind is in from the northeast
And the fog is setting in
Looks like I'll be having Christmas here
But it's time I should be in

Now the wind is very strong me boys
And the sea is mountains high
Nobody comes to pick me up
With this weather I'm gonna cry
I'm just like the Layaway
Nobody comes to get
And the helicopter is all fogged down
This Christmas, I'll never forget

So many disappointments boys
I've seen down through the years
Trying to get home for Christmas
And I haven't got a prayer
I pity some little children
If Santa was like me
There'd be no gifts for Christmas
Underneath the Christmas tree

It's Christmas Eve and the weather's still bad
And I've a pain called gout in my foot
My buddy's gone to cut a tree
And all he finds is a spruce
When Santa comes he'll be surprised
If he ever comes at all
He won't see much this Christmas
When down the chimney he falls

But we'll try to make the best of it
And spare the things we got
Some turkey and a little wine
But rum we have not
I'm sure we'll pay up for it
Whenever we get back home
And put all things aside
From this Christmas away from home

Chapter Two

The Fortune Bay Light

St. Jacques Island

Although St. Jacques Island in Fortune Bay is only a mile from the Newfoundland mainland, there were times when it might as well have been half way across the Atlantic. In high winds, there is no way to secure a boat to the rocks, especially in winter when ice coats the rocks like frozen glue.

Built in 1908, the St. Jacques lighthouse served the bustling marine traffic in Fortune Bay in the days of wooden ships and iron men. Besides the banking schooner crews, there have also been numerous rum-runners plying their trade from the French islands of St. Pierre and Miquelon who have thanked their lucky stars for the St. Jacques light. The fact that a ship has never foundered on St. Jacques Island since the lighthouse was established is, to a large extent, testimony to the success of the light.

Families like Evans, Penny, Burke, Hickey, Shepherd, Strowbridge, Fiander, Miles and others braved the isolation, the weather and the loneliness to serve. Most of them share common experiences and stories. All of them were concerned about what could happen if someone needed emergency medical attention when getting off the island was impossible in stormy weather.

Despite the isolation, most families have fond memories of life on St. Jacques Island. Betty Strowbridge lived there more than four years with her husband, Walt. Betty, who was raising two children almost by herself when her husband fished on deep-sea draggers, liked living in a lighthouse. "I was just happy to have Walt home after his being gone so much when he worked on the draggers in Nova Scotia," she said.

Storms are a frequent topic with lighthouse keepers. That's not surprising because bad weather is why there are lighthouses and lighthouse keepers. Lightkeepers who lived on St. Jacques Island grin when they talk about windstorms that routinely blew doors off hinges and windows out of buildings. Others tell about icing conditions caused by freezing spray that tore wooden railings from fence posts. They laugh when they say there has hardly ever been a flake of snow land on the island. When there is a snowfall, it seems the high winds that often accompany it refuse to let snow stop until it reaches more hospitable landing sites. Always, when St. Jacques lightkeepers talk of storms, they talk about the most vicious one of all — the one that claimed two of their own in 1963.

Storm of The Century

Erosion
E.J. Pratt
It took the sea a thousand years,
A thousand years to trace
The granite features of this cliff
In crag and scarp and base

It took the sea an hour one night,
An hour of storm to place
The sculpture of the granite seams
Upon a woman's face.

The loss of assistant lightkeepers Eric Fiander and Hughie Miles marks one of the saddest times in the history of the lighthouse perched on top of the rugged little island in Fortune Bay.

The principal lightkeeper, Hubert Miles, was ashore on leave when a powerful windstorm struck the area on December 19, 1963. Eric Fiander, aged twenty-five, who had worked at the lighthouse for nearly two years, was left in charge. Hubert Miles' seventeen-year-old nephew Hughie, an aspiring lightkeeper, went to the island to assist Eric in his lightkeeping duties during the Christmas period.

No one knows what happened to the two young men but Eric's

wife, Katherine Fiander, also twenty-five at the time, has vivid memories of the last day she saw her husband.

Courtesy Katherine Fiander

Katherine Fiander

The storm had swept across most of Atlantic Canada on that fateful Thursday, packing hurricane-force winds that whipped up mountainous seas. The Newfoundland coastal freighter *Mary Pauline* foundered in the seas near St. Pierre with the loss of six crewmembers. Another twelve men perished when the French vessel, *Douala* was battered to pieces on rocks near Burgeo. The storm also claimed the lives of six people on the land.

By Friday morning, the storm had hit Newfoundland's south coast in full fury with winds registered at 140 to 150 kilometres an hour with gusts to as high as 160. The raging seas and high winds created extremely bad freezing spray conditions. All windward sides of the lighthouse, the lightkeeper's residence and the storage shed were coated with ice six to eight inches thick.

At 11:00 a.m. Eric and Hughie went outside to inspect the forty-foot iron lighthouse tower and the fog alarm building. While they were out, the two men checked the boat landing where their dory was located. An hour later they returned with the news that the shed that housed their boat's engine and supplies had blown over. During lunch, the two men discussed their options and decided to try and secure the shed with a rope to keep the small building from blowing off the cliff into the ocean. Immediately after lunch they said goodbye to Katherine and headed out into the storm again.

Although the storm raged, Katherine was not afraid. She and Eric had lived on the island for nearly two years and this was not the first time she had heard the winds howl. Neither was it the first time Eric

Katherine and Eric Fiander with their two-week-old son Alton

Eric Fiander in the basement workshop of the lighthouse residence St. Jacques Island

had worked outdoors in stormy weather. With three small children aged one, two and three, she was busy preparing for Christmas, a few days away. Accustomed to rough weather, Katherine wasn't even thinking about Eric and Hughie until sometime around three o'clock when she heard Eric call out to her, seemingly from the basement. Even then she didn't think anything had gone wrong. Down the hallway from the basement door, Katherine was busy with the baby in one of the three bedrooms in the bungalow. Putting the baby down for an afternoon nap, she didn't even answer Eric's call for fear of waking the child. She didn't detect any sense of urgency in her husband's voice and decided she would go and see him in a few minutes after the baby fell asleep.

Assuming the men had come back from securing the shed and had gone downstairs, Katherine continued what she was doing until a few minutes later when she heard Eric call a second time.

"Katherine!" the voice called, this time much louder — this time, more like a nervous shout.

"What?" Katherine called back.

There was no reply. Katherine was still not worried and continued her work. Then suddenly, as if spooked, Katherine became alert and frightened. She listened uneasily for another call but the only thing she could hear was the howling of the wind. For a brief moment she wondered if she had really heard Eric's voice. Giving herself a mental shake she brushed aside those silly thoughts. "Of course I did," she said to herself. "They're downstairs." But still, somehow unconvinced, Katherine stopped what she was doing and cautiously went to check the basement.

"Eric," she called. "Eric, you down there?"

There was still no answer from Eric.

After walking slowly down the steps to confirm there was no one there, Katherine dismissed the notion that she'd even heard Eric call to her. Telling herself that her husband and his assistant were still attempting to secure the boat shed, Katherine kept working around the house all afternoon. Sometimes she found herself glancing toward the kitchen window but it was so heavily coated with ice, it was impossible to see anything outside. Even if she could see from the kitchen, the men were supposedly working by the landwash, a quarter mile from the house, below a cliff and far from her view. "Maybe the steep hill was too icy for them to climb," she reasoned. Perhaps they had secured the shed to its upright position and were staying inside it until weather and wind conditions improved. It wouldn't have been the first time Eric had done that.

Soon, Katherine faced a new dilemma. Darkness was closing in and she needed to start the generator to provide electricity for light. The generator was located at the edge of the cliff in a shed near the lighthouse but after taking one quick look outside, Katherine changed her mind. The fifty-foot lifeline that was rigged between the residence and the generator was coated with ice five or six inches thick, much too big and slippery to grasp. To venture out on the ice-coated rocks in hurricane-force winds without a lifeline would be nothing less than suicide. With the day's light quickly fading, Katherine was becoming increasingly anxious for her husband but she also had to worry about the children and herself without light in the house.

Darkness brought no relief from the winds that evening. The storm continued its fury unabated and although the children were snug in bed, the total blackness heightened Katherine's anxiety even more. Fears crowded in on her as she listened to the howling winds that were now so loud they muted the earlier sound of seas crashing against the cliffs. In total darkness, the winds sounded like angry shrieking demons, mocking her. Still she kept telling herself that everything would be fine as soon as the winds calmed down. Keeping her eyes glued to the windows searching for a light or some sign of Eric and Hughie, Katherine forgot to stoke the furnace. Sometime in the middle of the night, she realized she was getting very cold. By the time she went downstairs to refuel the coal furnace, the fire had totally gone out. Try as she would, Katherine could not get the hard coal to ignite again. Now, to add to her misery, she was faced with another hazard —bitter cold.

By Saturday afternoon, all warmth had escaped the house. That's when the first feelings of desperation flooded over her. Fearing for her children's safety, she had to try to get to the generator. If she could get the generator started, she would at least have power to run her electric kettle and hotplate to heat some food for the children. She would also have light. She also needed the generator running to try to make radio contact with the Coast Guard station in Burin to send

St. Jacques Island

a message explaining her plight.

Although the winds had dropped slightly, the ice-covered life-line was as treacherous as ever. Nevertheless, she held on to it and managed to creep across the cliff to the generator shed. The first thing she noticed was that snow had drifted into the shed and had covered the generator. The snow-covered batteries had weakened and, although she tried, Katherine had no idea how to pull the compression levers and do the other things she needed to do to start the generator manually. Finally, with her arms trembling from the strain of turning the engine, she gave up. Feeling more dejected and alone than ever, she somehow managed to fight her way back through the storm to the residence.

As Saturday's daylight started to slip into darkness Katherine frantically searched for a candle or anything that would give light. For the first time in thirty-six hours she was blessed with a tiny stroke of luck. She found an old kerosene lamp and although the flue was broken, it had enough oil to give a small light for the night. The tiny light somehow managed to give Katherine courage and even a bit of hope that things would turn out to be fine when the wind stopped. For a woman who had not eaten or slept for two days, Katherine felt tireless and, at times, even energetic.

Suddenly, a crashing noise sent her bolt upright. It sounded like the chimney had foundered. "If it was the chimney," she thought, "the roof would be next to go." But there was nothing Katherine could do except sit and watch and wait. All night she listened, her heart pounding in her chest.

Suddenly, the wind stopped. Maybe there was warning but if there was, Katherine doesn't remember it. One minute it was howling and then nothing — nothing but darkness and quiet. Strangely, the quiet was more unsettling than the wind. Now she had new expectations. It was almost as if the winds were an explanation and an excuse for everything that had gone wrong. Now it was quiet but there was still no sound of Eric and Hughie approaching the house. "What could be the problem now?" she wondered out loud.

Sunday's dawn opened a beautiful day. Katherine went outside expecting to see Eric and Hughie coming up the hill. Huge clumps of ice lying scattered over the ground explained the crashing noises from the previous night. The chimney was still in place but large pieces of ice, seven or eight inches thick, had fallen from the chimney onto the roof before sliding to the ground. Although she kept searching along the cliff, Katherine couldn't bring herself to go to the beach where Eric and Hughie were last headed. As long as she didn't know for sure, she could hope, and she knew that hope was the only thing keeping her from falling to pieces.

Around noon a small boat with several people onboard passed by the island. Katherine frantically waved a towel and yelled at the top of her voice trying to attract their attention, but no one saw her. Dejected and afraid, Katherine stayed outside, her eyes scouring the coastline and the island, searching for a sign of Eric and Hughie. Shortly after noon a wave of joy swept over her when she saw two men coming up the hill. At last, there they are! she thought. But her elation quickly vanished when she realized that it was not Eric and Hughie. Recognizing the men as Tom Osbourne and Roland Stoodley from St. Jacques, Katherine slowly accepted the inevitable — Eric was gone.

Deep inside she had known it all along — from the moment she heard him call her name on Friday afternoon.

A Double Tragedy

Tragedy struck early at the keepers of the St. Jacques light. Just eight years after the lighthouse was constructed in 1908, lighthouse keeper Isaac Burke died while carrying out a rescue mission.

Saturday, July 29, 1916 was a windy day in Fortune Bay. The brisk southerly wind came up quickly, catching a couple of vessels off guard as they approached Belloram and St. Jacques. One vessel made it to port but the other one, *Caribou*, was making little or no headway. The owner and master of the vessel, Phillip Ryan from Long Harbour, decided to anchor for the night in an area called Little Reach. Winds were still strong on Sunday morning but by early evening they had died down enough for Ryan to take another look. After sizing up the situation, Ryan and his travelling companion, Harry

Clinton, a social worker, decided to head for St. Jacques, a few miles to the southwest.

A couple of miles away, out on St. Jacques Island, lighthouse keeper Isaac Burke was keeping an eye on the *Caribou* as he watched the boat labouring heavily under the stiff offshore breeze. Just as Isaac trained his telescope on the boat for a closer look, a sudden gust of wind hit the *Caribou*, flipping over the small yacht as if it were a matchstick. Both Phillip Ryan and Harry Clinton were flung into the ocean. The lightkeeper dropped his telescope and, as quickly as he could, ran to the beach and launched his dory. There was no way he could row to the site where the *Caribou* had capsized so he decided to head for St. Jacques, a little more than a mile away. There, he thought, he could get a motorboat to go to the scene. As he rowed, Isaac figured that whoever was onboard the *Caribou* might have managed to get into one of the two lifeboats they had been towing.

As soon as he arrived at St. Jacques, Isaac went to see Dr. Conrad Fitzgerald who owned the most seaworthy vessel in the town. Knowing the brisk winds could cause problems, the doctor enlisted the help of George and Alexander Tibbo, both experienced fishermen from St. Jacques. Wanting to finish the rescue mission he started, Isaac Burke asked if he could go along too.

By the time the arrangements were made it was late in the evening, but darkness was not considered a major obstacle. Dr. Fitzgerald had piloted his boat, the *Albatross*, around Fortune Bay for forty years and knew the coastline like the back of his hand. From Isaac's description of the place and time of the accident, they decided that if there were survivors, they would probably have drifted to an area called Back Cove near Belloram.

An ominous wind whistled through the riggings of the *Albatross* as the four-man crew searched the ocean. There was no sign of either the *Caribou* or of Phillip Ryan and Harry Clinton. Hoping to provide a guide for the missing men in case they were nearby, Dr. Fitzgerald lit a lantern and hung it in the riggings of his boat as they slowly maneuvered the *Albatross* up and down the coastline near Back Cove.

Meanwhile, back on shore, word of the accident had spread quickly. Someone contacted the captain of the mail-steamer *S.S.*

Hump in Belloram to advise him of the incident. Captain Horwood didn't ask a lot of questions but quickly gathered a crew and headed his steamer to the search area where Issac Burke had seen the vessel capsize. Unfortunately, Captain Horwood was not informed that Dr. Fitzgerald was already in the area onboard the *Albatross*. Mistaking the lantern in the riggings of the *Albatross* for a possible light from the ill-fated *Caribou*, Captain Horwood headed straight for the light at full speed. It was too late when the crew of the *Hump* realized the light was smaller and much closer than they had first thought. The *Hump* smashed into the *Albatross,* slicing the doctor's boat in pieces, throwing Dr. Fitzgerald, Isaac Burke and Alexander and George Tibbo into the water. The doctor managed to climb into a small rescue boat which, miraculously, had come untied from the *Albatross* after the collision. He later managed to row to safety in Belloram, about a mile away. The two Tibbo men were rescued by crewmembers from the *Hump* but there was no sign of the lighthouse keeper Isaac Burke. It is thought he was killed instantly when the *Hump* hit the *Albatross* amidships.

Sadly, the loss of the man who witnessed the original accident was in vain. It is believed that Phillip Ryan and Harry Clinton were already dead at the time of the collision. Ironically, Isaac Burke's son, Charles, was steward on the *Hump* at the time of the double tragedy.

As in many tragic events in rural Newfoundland, that was not the end of the sorrow for the Burke family. Adrian Burke, one of Isaac Burke's sons, died just a few weeks after the accident. He was in his early twenties. Local legend has it that Adrian died from a "chill" caught on the very night of his father's death. Since people don't die from chills, that was probably a reference to pneumonia or other complications resulting from exposure.

Four years later, in 1920, another son, Dick, and a daughter, Adela, both in their early twenties, drowned while rowing to St. Jacques Island where their late father had worked as keeper of the light. Strangely, despite good weather conditions, an intensive search found no trace of the two. The only thing ever found by searchers was a shoe belonging to Adela.

Chapter Three

Icing on The Cape

South Head – Bay of Islands

Winds. Gale-force, storm-force and even hurricane-force winds are a fact of life for people who live and work in lighthouses. What most people characterize as a "windy day" is considered normal on exposed headlands, islands and capes around Newfoundland and Labrador. Even children factored the constant winds into their everyday life around lighthouses.

Michelle Myrick grew up at Cape Pine on the southern Avalon Peninsula. She says the wind usually determined what types of outdoor games they would play. "We had to be pretty creative in our playing. It was still the usual kid games like hide and seek — it's just that our hiding places were probably a bit more interesting — around the (light) tower you could go in circles for hours and never get caught. It all depended on how good your hearing was and how windy it was."

Pat (Patricia) Gillard remembers that it was always so windy on Belle Isle where she grew up that she never had light summer clothes. "Even on the warmest days in summer when my mother and I would go for a walk on the island in the afternoon, it would always be so windy and cool I could never wear shorts," she said.

Summer winds are one thing, but storm-force winds in winter are a constant worry for lighthouse people. Heavy winter winds are often accompanied by blinding snowstorms in the Northwest Atlantic. The same weather disturbance that causes the winds and snow usually creates heavy seas. Depending on temperatures, seas driven by extreme winds often cause an even more severe problem —

South Head — Bay of Islands

freezing spray. When huge waves crash against high rocky cliffs and headlands, the salt spray sometimes spouts as high as a hundred feet in the air. If temperatures are below the freezing point, spray turns to ice the instant it lands on rocks, buildings, wires or anything that's not heated.

Lightkeeper Brian Cull remembers a sleet storm on Little Burin Island in the 1980s. The entire island was coated in several inches of ice. "We were four days chopping notches in the ice in order to walk around outside the house," he says.

Max and Faith Sheppard know all about freezing spray. They saw enough of it one night in January, 1961 to last a lifetime.

Max was principal lightkeeper at South Head, Bay of Islands on Newfoundland's west coast the day he witnessed the worst storm that he had ever seen. Located about fifteen miles west of Corner Brook, the South Head lighthouse was perched at the very tip of the headland about ninety-five feet above the ocean.

January 15, 1961 was a fairly routine day for the six people at the lightstation. Max and the assistant lightkeeper, his cousin Wilson Sheppard, were working around the light tower until late afternoon. Faith and her young daughter Sheila were next door in the adjoining lightkeepers' residences visiting Wilson's wife Thelma and her seven-month-old child, Anna. The weather was what some New-foundlanders describe as "mauzy": overcast with light southerly winds and temperatures above freezing. As Faith described it "a gray, damp day but fairly mild for winter."

Around 4:00 p.m., Max and Wilson finished their work in the light tower and started fixing an outboard motor. As they worked, the men noticed the wind had suddenly changed direction. Almost instantly it shifted from the south and chopped to a brisk northwest-erly. A few minutes later the winds picked up to a stiff breeze and temperatures began to drop rapidly.

Faith also noticed the change in weather. Because Thelma lived in the leeward side of the house, Faith knew the weather would be much worse on the front of the duplex where she lived. As she chatted with Thelma, she began to feel uneasy about the change in weather. She didn't have four-year-old Sheila dressed appropriately because it had been warm when she left her house. "I think I'd better get ready to go back home before the weather gets any worse," Faith said to Thelma as she started dressing her child. By the time she was ready to leave, Faith was so worried about the winds that she thought she should carry her daughter. Although it was only about twenty feet from Thelma's door to her own, Faith called out to Max to give her a hand. Already, the wind was so strong that Faith had to walk cautiously, bracing herself to keep from being blown against the house.

With Faith and Sheila safely at home, Max decided to make all the regular checks on the lighthouse in case the storm got worse. With that done he and Wilson returned to their respective homes to keep an eye on the storm from there. Wilson was on evening watch so Max decided to get some sleep before starting his watch at midnight. There was something about the look of the sky and the feel of the wind that twigged a sixth sense about weather that lightkeepers and mariners seem to have. This could be a long night, he thought. He was right.

As winds continued to grow stronger all evening, the seas got rougher. By 8:00 p.m. the waves were smashing against South Head so violently that water and spray were coming to the top of the cliff, landing no more than a few yards away from Max and Faith's door. By nine o'clock, spray was soaring more than a hundred feet over the top of the cliff, sending water closer and closer to the house. By then, the temperature had dropped dramatically and the cold saltwater spray was turning to ice as soon as it hit the ground.

As the wife of a lighthouse keeper, Faith Sheppard had spent many winter evenings listening to winds howl as seas crashed against the cliffs. In her four years on South Head she had also watched snow whipped around by winds lashing at her windows. But this storm was different. This time, instead of snow beating at her windows, it was freezing spray and it was building quickly. By ten o'clock several inches of ice had formed on the windows, making it impossible to see out. But still Faith didn't worry. She wondered about the weight of the ice and if it was reaching the roof, but as she puts it today, "I was young then and never worried much about anything."

Faith's calm was abruptly shattered at 10:30 p.m. The living room was suddenly filled with smoke. "Thick black smoke was pouring through the stovepipe into the room so I knew right away something was wrong," she says. Faith had no fear of winds and heavy seas but she freely admits to having a terrible fear of fire. Not stopping to investigate, Faith jumped from her chair and ran upstairs to wake her husband. "On the way along, I pounded on the kitchen wall to alert Wilson and Thelma that something might be wrong," she remembers. There were no telephones in either residence and because of frequent stormy weather on South Head, the two families had devised a system of signals in case they wanted to communicate without going outdoors. A good hard knock on the adjoining kitchen walls was a signal to get all ears close to the wall for a message, which would be yelled out.

After he doused the fire with water, Max went outdoors to see

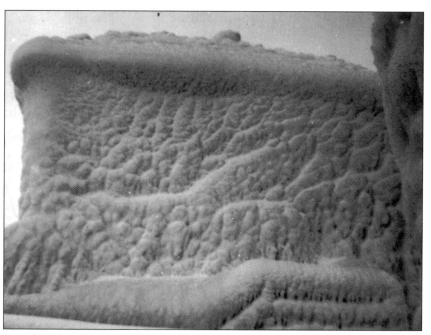

Lighthouse residence after a freezing spray storm on South Head in 1961.

what caused the stove to smoke. It didn't take long to figure it out. Spray from the heavy seas was going all the way to the roof, carrying with it slob ice filled with thousands of pieces of ocean debris. The slob and debris had gone down the chimney, clogging the stovepipe. Wilson, still on lighthouse watch at the time, joined Max outside the house. The two lightkeepers decided there was nothing they could do about the chimney while the storm raged.

While they were out they figured they might as well check the lighthouse. The clock would soon need winding to keep the light rotating and, as always during a bad storm, it was safer for both men to go together. The door to the lighthouse was heavily coated with ice but they managed to get it open wide enough to see inside. One look told them to go no farther. The winds and ice had smashed out several panes of window in the lighthouse tower. The light itself would probably be next to go. It was far too dangerous to try to provide makeshift repairs that night. There was nothing the men could do but go back to their families and wait out the storm.

When Max returned from the light tower, Faith informed him

that Thelma had invited them to spend the night at their house. Without the coal stove functioning, the house was already growing cold so Max agreed that spending the night with their neighbours was a good idea, especially for their daughter. Faith packed a supply of food in a flour sack to take with them in case the storm lasted a day or more. By 1:30 a.m., they had everything, including Sheila, ready to go. Faith even had her "cash box" in the flour sack with the rest of her supplies. "I wasn't taking any chances on losing anything in case something happened to the house," she said.

Preparing to brave the storm, Max knew the door was going to be difficult to open. Two hours had passed since he had come back from the lighthouse and the storm had gotten worse. He couldn't see through the ice-covered windows but he somehow sensed that the freezing spray was getting thicker and heavier. He also knew the spray was shooting farther up over the house. Although he knew the storm had deepened, Max was surprised to find that he couldn't even move the door. At first he thought the force of the wind was too heavy against the door, but it wouldn't move even when the winds subsided for a few moments. It was only then that Max realized ice had built up so thick that the door was frozen shut. It would be impossible to open it, perhaps for days.

Pondering their next move, Max and Faith knew that now, more than ever, they had to get out of the house. If the storm got worse, the increasing weight from ice build-up could crush the roof, trapping them inside. With the only door to the outside covered in hundreds of pounds of ice, there was no easy way out. Despite their predicament, no one panicked. They knew that if push came to shove, they could beat a hole through a wall to the adjoining house, but that would only be necessary in case of dire emergency.

Suddenly Max had an idea. If they could climb through a hatch in a clothes closet in one of the upstairs bedrooms, maybe they could crawl across the ceiling joists to another hatch in a bedroom in Wilson and Thelma's house. Knocking on the kitchen wall to get his neighbours' attention, Max called out his plan. Getting through the 24" x 18" hatch would be a tight squeeze but, with nothing to lose, everyone agreed it was worth a try.

As Max and Faith got their daughter ready, Wilson opened the hatch and shone a light through to the attic so his friends could see where to go. Careful to take everything she considered valuable, including food and cash box, Faith went first. After she made it through the small hatch, Faith slowly crawled across the rafters, careful not to place her weight in the wrong place — one wrong move and she would go crashing down through the ceiling. Slowly Faith edged her way along the 2" x 4" ceiling joists until finally she made it to the hatch in the adjoining dwelling. Max and Sheila followed, and a few minutes later all three of them were safe and comfortable in the warmth of their friends' home on the leeward side of the storm.

The storm raged and the seas pounded South Head all that night as the two lightkeepers and their wives stayed awake, nervously watching for signs of anything that might go wrong. None of them had ever seen a storm as vicious as this one.

Although isolated and alone, the four felt a small level of comfort as they listened to the marine radio communications on the VHF radio set throughout the night. But sometime in the early morning hours, the outdoor antenna crashed to the ground under the weight of ice. Without the VHF, their link to the outside world was severed so Max immediately started working on an alternate plan. By late morning he had jerryrigged an antenna from small pieces of discarded wire and attached it to the radio set. There was nothing sophisticated about it, but the makeshift antenna worked. While they waited for the storm to end, Max successfully made contact with a marine radio operator in Corner Brook and informed him of their plight. "He could barely hear me, but he made out what I was saying, that was the main thing," Max said.

Finally, at approximately two-thirty the next afternoon, the winds dropped enough for Max and Wilson to go outside and inspect the place. They could hardly believe their eyes. The west and northwest facing sides of the lighthouse, the residence and the foghorn building were covered in solid ice nearly four feet thick. The front bridge to the head lightkeeper's residence looked like a beach in winter. Seaweed, pieces of wood, rocks and, amazingly, hundreds

South Head lighthouse buildings coated in 3.5 feet of ice in January, 1961.

of small fish were strewn everywhere. There were even dead fish on the roof of the house. A dory that had been hauled up near the lighthouse was missing. The only thing remaining was the stem of the boat still attached by rope through a ringbolt fastened to a post. Obviously the weight of the water and ice in the dory had been too much for the stem to hold. Wilson and Max never did find a trace of the dory or the outboard motor that was stored in it.

After determining there was nothing more they could do until help arrived to chop the ice from the buildings, Max went back to the house to tell the women to come out and take a look around. "You're not going to believe it," he told them.

Thelma went first while Faith stayed with the children. When Thelma returned Faith asked her what she thought of the situation. Thelma, known for her sense of humour, just looked at Faith and said, "Well, well, well, it's a wonder we hadn't all been crushed straight to hell under that weight."

Laughing, Faith replied "Well girl, I thought we might have gone somewhere last night but I didn't think it would be there."

It took three men nearly a week to chop the ice from the lightstation buildings that winter. Max Sheppard spent many more years as lightkeeper, mostly at the Point Amour lighthouse in Labrador, but he never saw another storm as bad as that one at South Head in January, 1961.

The Longest Night of My life

Four years later, Wilson and Melissa Kendell, along with lightkeeper Howard Sheppard, got a firsthand taste of what the storm of 1961 was like.

An intense winter storm had battered the South Head lighthouse all day on February 12, 1965. Although the storm hadn't caused any damage, Wilson and his fellow lightkeeper, Howard Sheppard kept a close eye on things, just in case it got worse. Wilson and Melissa went to bed about 10:30 p.m. as Howard started the night shift. The next thing Melissa remembers is being awakened from a deep sleep by the sound of Howard's voice calling from the foot of the stairs. "Wilson, get up — it's getting really rough and water is coming in around the doors and windows."

Melissa recalls jumping out of bed and hearing the sound of seas pounding against the side of the house. At the foot of the stairs Melissa saw small rivers of seawater running across the floor, collecting in pools near the centre of the living room. Rushing to get pails and mops, the three started what Melissa later described as "the longest night of my life." As seas continued to pound against the side of the house, Melissa was relieved that, at least her four children were sleeping soundly in the upstairs bedrooms, undisturbed by the thumps and hisses of the seas retreating from the outside walls of the house every other minute. "I remember a shudder going through my whole body, every time a sea broke over the house, afraid something would give way to the tremendous weight of the water."

As the two lightkeepers and Melissa mopped and threw water down the kitchen sink, they wondered if the men should try to rewind the manually operated light. As water started freezing on the

South Head Lighthouse and buildings after a massive winter storm in 1925.

house, they soon realized there was no way to get to the light tower that night. "It probably doesn't matter anyway; it's too rough for ships to be on the coast tonight," Howard said. Fifteen minutes later, all three were stunned to see the lights of a ship passing the lighthouse, heading towards open seas. Later, they learned that the ship had been docked at a wharf in Corner Brook that was damaged by the rough seas. The ship's captain decided it was safer to "jog" into the storm at sea than take a chance on becoming grounded in the Bay of Islands.

Though curious about why a ship would venture out to sea that night, Howard and Wilson were satisfied the ship seemed safe and went back to the job at hand. They knew they had to keep the saltwater from flooding the basement where their freshwater supply was stored in a large reservoir. As the men and Melissa worked, they talked about the storm of 1961. They had all heard the story of Max and Faith Sheppard's adventure. During that conversation, someone mentioned freezing spray going down the chimney, dousing the fire. That's when Howard and Wilson decided to feed the coal furnace at double the normal rate. They figured that a roaring fire would keep the chimney hot enough to keep ice from forming at the top. They were right. While ice continued to build up on the front of the house, providing a form of insulation from the howling winds, the roaring fire kept everyone warm.

Melissa recalls that when she stopped to rest a few minutes, she thought how calm and controlled her husband and Howard were that night. They toiled, non-stop, always focused on what they had to do without a word of complaint or concern that they couldn't stay ahead of the seas, although there were times the water was gaining on them. Watching the men, Melissa was reminded of a quote from Winston Churchill she heard when she was a young girl. According to the famous British Prime Minister, "It is a mistake to look too far ahead. Only one link in the chain of destiny can be handled at a time."

Encouraged by her thoughts, Melissa found new strength and rejoined the men as they mopped and dumped water all night. Finally, at about 4:00 a.m., the seas receded a little and water stopped pouring into the house. An eternity later, at dawn, the men managed to get a door open wide enough to squeeze outside. As in the storm four years previous, ice had coated everything. Without even taking time for a nap, Howard and Wilson started what turned out to be a week-long cleanup operation.

Chapter Four

The Light in the Devil's Mouth

Cape Anguille

Cape Anguille can be very deceptive.

Jutting out into the Gulf of St. Lawrence at the entrance to St. George's Bay, the cape is located on the tip of one of the most picturesque places in Newfoundland. In summer, tourists who fancy themselves creative photographers love to snap rolls of pictures of the fifty-eight-foot high pyramid-shaped wooden lighthouse sitting at the foothills of the Anguille Mountains. Expecting to find lighthouses always perched on rugged rocky headlands, people are surprised to find a marine beacon located on the edge of a gently sloping grassy meadow. At first glance, the Cape Anguille lighthouse defies all the stereotypical expectations of visitors. Not only is the cape at the lower end of a meadow, it's also situated in the town of Codroy, a farming community of approximately 1000 people, located at the southern tip of St. George's Bay.

On a calm summer day, Cape Anguille is a photographer's dream. On a stormy winter night, it is a mariner's worst nightmare. The same swooping hills that provide a beautiful backdrop for snapshots also cause some of the most bizarre weather behaviour on the east coast of Canada.

Cape Anguille, the most westerly point of land on the island of Newfoundland, has been battered by the most vicious winds imaginable. Local fishermen and other weather watchers say winds, especially from the southeast and southwest, surf up the mountains. The angle of the mountains, in turn, causes winds to curl backwards toward the ocean with dramatic effects on wind directions and

Cape Anguille

patterns. Fishermen say when the winds swoop down from the mountains, it's not unusual to experience high winds from several directions at once, creating serious problems for vessels of all sizes. Under normal stormy conditions, skippers point their vessels directly into the wind and reduce engine power to the level where it is just enough to keep the boat from moving in any direction. In most cases they can "jog" or head into the storm and ride it out until conditions improve. But when heavy winds slam them from several directions at once, they lose control over their ships.

Compounding the danger to vessels when confused weather conditions occur, it is also common to experience a phenomenon known as "waterspouts." Waterspouts are the marine equivalent of tornadoes. Rarely more than 600 feet wide at sea level, they are rapidly churning funnels of wind swirling up to hundreds of feet above the water. Waterspouts move slowly over the ocean and, like tornadoes, they have an average life span of only eight or nine minutes. The spout rotates rapidly above the ocean surface in a zigzag path that almost always leaves turbulent seas in its wake. Fishermen near Cape Anguille have seen several waterspouts at once within a five-mile radius.

Perhaps the Anguille Mountains are to blame for another weather peculiarity in St. George's Bay. For some reason, high winds often strike with alarming speed. It's almost as if a weather system pounces on the sea from out of nowhere. Even when wind warnings have been issued by Environment Canada Weather Services, storms often hit suddenly, creating tremendous turmoil in the ocean. In fact, seas in the area are "officially" recognized as being treacherous in stormy conditions. The Newfoundland Sailing Directions state:

> The flood tidal stream is usually North-going and the ebb stream South-going; frequently there are heavy tide rips between Cape Anguille and Codroy Island. During stormy weather, there is a heavy and confused sea in this area. . .

Because of its environmental peculiarities, mariners and fishermen have given the mouth of Bay St. George nicknames. During a vicious storm in the early 1940s, the cargo vessel *Fenmore* had to be abandoned when taking on water after developing a serious list several miles from the cape. Crewmembers on board the rescue vessel *Foundation Josephine* had such a struggle battling heavy seas and high winds they named the bay The Forbidden Sea. In more recent years, mariners refer to the area as The Devil's Mouth, a reference to both the giant mouth-like shape of St. George's Bay and the ferocious winds that swoop down from the Anguille Mountains. Weather like that, they say, can only come from the mouth of the devil himself.

Because of unpredictable storms, many ships have been lost near Cape Anguille.. In the early 1900s, pressure was mounting on governments to establish a light there. Following the loss of the cargo ship *Mary Otis* near the cape in 1904, the Quebec government decided to build a lighthouse with equipment and parts supplied by France. The French built the light to assist their shipping interests sailing from the lower north shore of Quebec to Halifax and to the French islands of St. Pierre and Miquelon, fourteen miles off the south coast of Newfoundland. The west coast of Newfoundland was also a prime fishing area for a large French fishing fleet at the turn of the century.

Eel or Plateau?

Whether the cape was named after the mountain range or vice versa is not known. "Anguille" is a French word with several meanings, including "eel." St. George's Bay has always been home to the biggest eel fishery in the province. There are stories of aboriginal people on the west coast, hundreds of years ago, spearing eels for food. "Anguille" is also used by the French to describe what Newfoundland fishermen know as a slipway. A "slip," as it is also called, is constructed of logs nailed together and laid directly on a beach, especially in exposed rocky areas where there is little or no sand. Fishermen haul their boats from the water to the security of the slipway out of reach of the ocean's waves. Fishermen around Cape Anguille would have had slips for their small boats before the construction of large wharves in more recent times.

"Anguille" can also be used in French to describe a plateau. The Anguille Mountain Range is well known for its flat top, leading some people to think the mountains were named for that characteristic, and the cape named after the mountains.

The Robin Hood of the Cape

In eighty-five years of staffed operation there were only three principal lightkeepers on Cape Anguille. The first was Alfred Patry from Quebec. Laurier Patry succeeded his father in the 1950s, and Henry Reid took over as principal keeper from 1984 until the light became automated in 1990.

For more than half its existence, the lighthouse at Cape Anguille was the personal domain of one man. Alfred Patry became principal lightkeeper when the light was established in 1905, a job he held until his retirement in the 1950s.

The Frenchman from Quebec became one of the best known

Courtesy Canadian Coast Guard, Fisheries and Oceans

Alfred Patry (1927), lightkeeper, Cape Anguille

characters in the Codroy Valley. People from the valley still talk about him today, nearly fifty years after his retirement. Afraid of nothing, Patry has been described as everything from "a crazy old bastard" to "a small man with a great big heart."

No matter how people perceived Alfred Patry, they never forgot the man known for his boundless energy. Patry was a self-taught ironworker, welder, carpenter, electrician, historian and communicator extraordinaire. A well-read man, Patry was a passionate debater. Never one to back down from a good argument, the lighthouse keeper didn't care who challenged him, according to Bert Downey from O'Regans in the Codroy Valley. "Politicians, community leaders, even clergy, — they were all the same to Alfred Patry; he'd take them all on and tell them exactly what he thought of them and their points of view." Merchants were always under his scrutiny.

Patry's zest for a good argument was equalled only by his drive to help the local people to improve themselves. Always urging

Principal lightkeeper's dwelling, Cape Anguille (1944), Alfred Patry's car in front.

people to strive to do more, Alfred Patry practised what he preached. Retired lighthouse keeper Henry Reid says Patry never asked people to do anything he didn't think they could accomplish and rarely did he ask them to do anything he couldn't do himself. "If he pushed you to do something, whether it was something physical or whatever, he'd join you in the struggle until you succeeded." Patry dared people to be different and lived his own life as an example of an independent and forward-thinking person. He was one of the first people in the Valley area to own a car — a 1944 Dodge Coupe. Some say he was also the first person there to own a television.

Patry was close friends with people from all walks of life. Although he had a tendency to be brash at times, there was also a flare of elegance about him. He owned several racehorses, including one called Red Maude, and often entertained wealthy and powerful people from Quebec and other parts of Canada in the large six-bedroom home he built near the lighthouse.

Some people suggest that Patry may have entertained his guests with ample supplies of "beverages" hidden for months in the carefully configured walls of the big house in the meadow. Legend has it that the plucky little lightkeeper thought it fair game to "safeguard" a few bottles of contraband booze from time to time. One never knew when a medical emergency might occur, especially in a lighthouse. Hot brandy was known in those days for its tremendous medicinal attributes. Hundreds of mariners will attest to being snatched from the jaws of death by a wee sip of life-giving brandy after being rescued from a treacherous ocean. Alfred Patry, it seems, was always prepared to prescribe a drink of brandy for a variety of ailments, if called upon.

Despite his argumentative demeanour, his eccentricities and his friendship with the well-to-do, Alfred Patry was best known as a man with a kind heart. If anyone needed an electrical appliance or a piece of machinery repaired, he or she knew where to go. If a fisherman needed a hand to launch a boat, he could always call the lightkeeper for help. If a farmer in the valley fell on hard times, Alfred Patry would be the first to organize an assistance program. As often as not, Patry did favours that personally cost him considerable sums of money but he never charged a nickel, especially if it was for a farmer or fisherman. "He was always there for the little person; it didn't matter to him if you were a prince or a pauper, everyone was treated exactly the same," says Henry Reid.

Patry's employer never knew, or perhaps turned a blind eye, but the veteran lightkeeper often made it a point to order more supplies than were needed for the lighthouse. But no one in the Codroy Valley has ever suggested that Alfred Patry, the father of sixteen children, personally benefitted a single penny's worth. Patry seemed to always find a way to spread a surplus, if there was one, among needy people in surrounding communities. As someone in the valley once said, he was a kind of modern day Robin Hood of the Cape.

Beyond the Call of Duty

Like their colleagues nearly everywhere, lighthouse keepers at Cape Anguille have been called upon to rescue fishermen on numerous occasions. Henry Reid helped three fishermen to safety in the nick of time one day in the 1960s. Like most lightkeepers, Henry is not the kind of person who makes a fuss about rescuing a person from disaster, so he doesn't bother to remember exactly when the incident occurred.

It was in the spring, he says, probably in the mid-1960s. Winds were light that day but it was very foggy. Henry and a friend, Tom Gale, were getting ready to come ashore from hauling their salmon nets near the cape when they heard what they thought was a fishing boat nearby. There was something about the sound of the engine that caused the lightkeepers to pay attention. Henry described it as a loud thumping noise, but nothing they could distinguish as the sound of a vessel in distress. Thinking that perhaps it was merely the thick fog disguising the normal sounds of a fishing vessel, Henry and Tom set their last net and headed for shore. Just as they were hauling up their flat-bottomed dory near the lighthouse, Henry saw a small longliner. Although he couldn't get a good look at the vessel through the fog, Henry sensed there was something wrong. "That boat don't look right to me," he said to Tom.

Peering through the fog to get a better look, both men soon realized that the boat was the one making the strange sounds they'd heard. When the fog curled skyward off the water for a moment, Henry and Tom saw that the vessel was on fire.

Trying to rescue people from a burning boat at sea is a tricky business, and both Tom and Henry knew they would have to be careful. Undaunted by the danger, they quickly launched their dory to provide whatever assistance they could. Their first job was to get the burning vessel to a safe landing area on the shoreline. "We waved and shouted at the three fishermen on the boat to follow us to where we knew there was a safe spot to land but they must have been too anxious or too frightened because they paid no attention to us. Instead, they headed around the cape toward the worst possible place they could have gone because of all the rocks in the area," Henry said.

When the engine on the burning boat stopped operating, Henry feared the worst. If the boat drifted onto the rocks, it would be impossible to get the crew into the dory. But luck was with the fishermen that day. The winds were light and the seas were calm, giving them a few minutes grace. Before the fishing vessel could drift on top of the rocks, the three fishermen heeded the advice of Henry and Tom and gave up trying to salvage their boat and launched a small life raft. Working feverishly, Henry and Tom threw a towline to the raft and managed to get the fishermen safely away from the rocks and the burning boat. And not a second too soon either, according to Henry. "We had just got clear of the longliner when several drums of gasoline onboard caught fire and exploded; it was like a bomb going off."

Arriving at the lighthouse, Henry took the three men to the medical clinic in Codroy. Although suffering from minor burns and bruises, none were considered seriously hurt and were permitted to travel. But travel became the next problem for the three fishermen. All were from Rose Blanche, several hours away, over winding gravel road. Without a car or access to public transportation, the men were stranded. In the tradition of lighthouse keepers going far beyond the call of duty to help someone in need, Henry took care of everything and made arrangements to get the men to Rose Blanche. After consulting with the lightkeeper in Rose Blanche-Colombier Island, Henry volunteered to take the men to Wreckhouse, about halfway to Rose Blanche. At Wreckhouse, the men were picked up by the lightkeeper from Colombier Island who took them home.

Happy to be back in the comfort of their homes, the three fishermen were extremely grateful to the lightkeeper and his friend for not only taking care of them, but also for saving their lives. If Henry Reid and Tom Gale hadn't been able to get the fishermen away from the stricken vessel as soon as they did, there is no doubt all three men would have been killed in the explosion.

High Flying Lights

More than lighthouse keepers and their assistants got a taste of Cape Anguille's windy furore. A building contractor who worked on the construction of the current lighthouse in the 1960s got a firsthand look at the power of Bay St. George's winds. The contractor ordered that building materials for the new lighthouse be stored in a pile near the construction site. Anticipating there might be severe winds before the lighthouse was completed, an assistant lightkeeper told the contractor the building materials were not properly piled to withstand an Anguille windstorm. The contractor laughed at the man, saying he had constructed lighthouses all across Atlantic Canada and no wind could move the weight of those materials. "There is no need to talk about such foolishness as that," said the contractor. "Fine sir, whatever you say," the assistant lightkeeper replied, going quietly about his duties.

The contractor should have heeded the advice of the young lightkeeper. Three days later there was hardly a piece of lumber to be found near the cape. A strong, but not uncommon, southeasterly wind ripped through the area overnight, tossing the building materials around like popsicle sticks. It took several days before workers gathered the lumber that had been strewn over a one-mile radius. Some pieces were blown out to sea and never recovered. When the contractor arrived on the scene the next morning, he just stood there scratching his head muttering, "Where in God's name am I?"

By the Seat of Your Pants

Because tragedy often accompanies extreme winds, most lighthouse keeper's storm-stories are solemn tales. But Henry Reid laughs when he tells about one of the wildest winter nights he ever saw on Cape Anguille. Nonchalant about it all, Henry doesn't even remember what year it was, and the only thing damaged was Henry's rear end. "It was around 1982," he says, smiling at what he's about to tell. Henry and his family were living at the principal lightkeeper's residence on the cape. The residence was a large house about 400 feet inland from the light tower and the fog alarm building situated near the edge of the cliff. Just after supper one windy evening, it was time to check the foghorn to make sure it was operating properly. A light snow had changed to sleet as temperatures edged up to slightly above freezing. Henry had barely stepped off the front steps when a strong gust of wind sent him tumbling to the ground. The next thing he knew, the wind was pushing him over the icy ground as if he weighed no more than an empty pop can. "It was unbelievable," Henry laughs. "I managed to twist around to a sitting position and when the wind hit my back I was sailing down the incline toward the light tower and the bank, and there was absolutely nothing I could do but hope for the best." The image of a 175-pound man sliding on his behind across 500 feet of slippery ground is funny in retrospect, but as Henry got closer to the edge of a steep bank, it was no laughing matter. "I kept trying to dig my heels into the snow to slow myself down so I wouldn't get hurt too badly, but the wind was driving me so fast I couldn't break my speed at all." After sliding all the way past the fog alarm building, Henry's speed finally slowed when he reached two air tanks near a fence at the edge of the embankment. Grabbing the wire fence, Henry hung on until a lull in the winds allowed him to crawl to the fog alarm building. Once safely inside, he spent the next several hours waiting out the storm before attempting to go back to the residence, something he had done on many previous occasions.

Although it's a funny story today, Henry was very fortunate the fence was there and that he was able to curb his speed long enough to catch hold of something. Otherwise, he would have slipped over the thirty-foot embankment, ending up on icy rocks far enough below to cause serious injury. With several inches of slippery ice coating the rocks, it would have been impossible for Henry to get back to the top of the cliff that night.

The Devil of a Storm

January 24, 1987 was a day when Henry Reid, and many fishermen, felt that the mouth of Bay St. George lived up its nickname, Devil's Mouth. Although there was a wind warning issued, the day started with little more than a moderate northerly breeze accompanied by occasional snow flurries. The weather continued that way for most of the day as Henry worked his eight-hour shift from 9:00 a.m. to 5:00 p.m. In the late afternoon, the forecast gale-force southwesterly winds struck so suddenly that even long-time fishermen were caught off guard. So was Henry Reid. The veteran lightkeeper arrived home in Codroy shortly after five o'clock that evening.The weather was still fair when his wife Ruth met him in the porch to ask if he could pick up their daughter at school. As Henry turned to go back to the car, a sudden wind struck the house with such force that it startled both Henry and Ruth.

Henry's many years of experience observing weather and wind conditions told him to be cautious, even though only moments earlier the weather was, in Henry's words, "civil and quiet." Going outside, Henry was surprised to be fighting such high winds. He'd seen stronger winds but he couldn't remember when. "It was a struggle to stand up, the wind was that strong," he remembers, noting that there have been times on the cape when the winds were so strong that he couldn't stand. After picking up his daughter, Henry headed straight for home. "It was not an evening you wanted to hang around outside."

Although he was not on duty, the lighthouse keeper's first thoughts were of fishermen who might be caught off guard by the storm's sudden arrival. From conversations among fishermen he had overheard on the VHF radio at the lighthouse that day, Henry knew there were about a dozen fishing vessels just off the coast that evening. Instinctively, he went to his living room window, where he had a good view of the ocean, to see if any of the boats were still out. "It was a strange sight," he says. "The storm was low – right down on the water — I could see the winds churning just above the surface, but a few feet above the masts of the boats, it appeared like there was hardly any wind at all."

The storm grew worse that evening. Adding to the misery of fishing crews who were trying desperately to reach port, the temperature quickly dropped to ten degrees below freezing. Freezing spray soon turned to ice, causing the vessels to become dangerously top-heavy. On top of that, the flurries changed to heavy snow around six o'clock, reducing visibility to nil. Most of the fishermen made it safely to port at Codroy but the storm took its toll on two fishing vessels that night. One vessel, *Barry and Trina,* ran aground just a couple of miles south of Cape Anguille. Someone on the stricken vessel managed to get a lifeline to the shore, and all six crewmembers made it to safety on Codroy Beach. Another vessel would not be so fortunate.

The inshore dragger, *Myers III*, out of Bartlett's Harbour on Newfoundland's northwest coast, fought heavy seas, blinding snow, and freezing spray for several hours trying to make it to port in Codroy. But sometime around nine o'clock the forty-five-foot wooden vessel, heavily laden with fish, succumbed to the relentless pounding of the winds and seas. In what is now remembered as one of the saddest tragedies in the history of the Newfoundland inshore fishery, all five crewmembers, four of them brothers, perished. Sadly, they had almost made it to port. On May 26, 1987, the wreck of the *Myers III* was found on the bottom slightly more than a mile from the Codroy wharf.

Chapter Five

Point of Love or Cove of Death

P oint Amour is located in southern Labrador at the closest point to the island of Newfoundland, fourteen miles across the Strait of Belle Isle from Flowers Cove. On a sunny day, it visually lives up to it's French name. It is a lovely place. Lovely, that is, unless you were trying to manoeuvre a ship through the Strait in winter or on a foggy day, especially in the era before sophisticated navigational technology. In those days, the Point of Amour was all too often the Point aux Morts (Point of Death). Some people believe Point Amour was, in fact, originally named L'Anse aux Morts meaning Cove of Death or Point Mort, referring to death, so-named because of the large number of shipwrecks in the area. In a 1990 book entitled *Just One Interloper After Another,* author David Whalen wrote:

> Many a terrible sea disaster is part of the story of southern Labrador. With its dangerous iron bound coast of rocks and shoals, the narrow Strait of Belle Isle has probably claimed more ships per nautical mile of coastline than any other.

Other than dense fog which frequently blankets the Strait of Belle Isle, mariners have been threatened with a less obvious danger — strong ocean currents. Fishermen say currents in the area are so strong they have trouble steaming against them at times. In 1888, Rt. Reverend Michael Howley crossed the Straits near Point Amour and later wrote:

The great strength of the currents and tides which run past
here at a furious rate, making a rough sea when opposed
to the wind. They run three or four knots and, in winter,
carry ice pans as fast as a man can run.

Ocean currents can have an insidious effect on ships. They
silently push vessels of all shapes and sizes far off course without
warning. Fooled by the deceiving currents, hundreds of unsuspect-
ing mariners have been shocked to find themselves hard aground on
the jagged limestone reefs just off Point Amour.

Despite the danger, European explorers sailed through the Strait
of Belle Isle in the early 1500s. Even then it was recognized as the
great northern gateway to the Gulf of St. Lawrence. However, word
of the treacherous ocean currents, and dense fog and icebergs in
winter and spring, convinced most of them to take the less dangerous, albeit much longer, route around southern Newfoundland.
Later, with the introduction of steam-powered ships in the early
nineteenth century; mariners began attempting the "Gateway to
Canada" again. By the mid-1800s, shipping through the Straits had
reached a level whereby both the British Admiralty and the French
government in Quebec recognized the need for a series of lighthouses along the coasts of Labrador and Quebec. Francois Baby from
Quebec built the fourth and final light in the series at Point Amour in
1855.

One of the most magnificent lighthouses on the North American
continent, Point Amour took nearly four years to build. Constructed
of limestone, the second tallest light in Canada is twenty-five feet
wide at its base. Rising to the height of a ten-story office building, 125
feet to the top of the tower, the Point Amour lighthouse boasts 123
steps to the base of the lamp. There are another sixteen steps to the
top of the light. There are eight landings along the way. Climbing the
spiralling stairs, visitors can view the fabulous Labrador scenery
through one of the eight windows strategically located at each
landing. Jeff Wyatt, who spent forty-four years working at the Point
Amour lighthouse, estimated he climbed those stairs at least ten
thousand times.

Courtesy Canadian Coast Guard, Fisheries and Oceans

Point Amour Lighthouse

The limestone masonry at the base of the lighthouse tower proved inadequate to withstand the salt sea air, and within three years from opening date there were cracks in the mortar. The government then decided to cover the limestone with oak planks and cedar shingles to protect the limestone. Even that proved inadequate to totally protect the mortar on the side of the tower facing the ocean. That side of the lighthouse was eventually covered with firebrick.

With all the additional coverings, the walls of the huge lighthouse ultimately grew to be six feet thick. Because the structure at the base of the tower is so massive, visitors to the lighthouse today often feel they are entering a fortress.

Located on the edge of a sixty-foot high grassy ridge, the tall white light with the fifteen-foot black ring around it can be seen for miles. Today the light is fully automated and has become a major tourist attraction. Young men and women, mostly university students, dressed in turn-of-the-century costume, greet visitors at the entrance to the former lightkeeper's residence attached to the tower. A few brave souls accept the challenge of climbing the steep wooden stairs while most are content to stand at the base of the tower and just look up to the top of the massive light.

While the tremendous height of the Point Amour light is one of its main attractions, especially for tourists, it's questionable whether architects were more interested in aesthetic values or practicality. Situated on top of a sixty-foot bank, a light half that height would have been sufficient as a navigational aid.

Bobby Davis remembers a time when the height of the Point Amour tower was a safety concern. Bobby's teen-aged brother single-handedly fought a fire at the top of the stairs. Carrying water in buckets from the lighthouse residence, he found the 125 steps almost insurmountable after a few trips.

It was just before Christmas, 1934. Bobby's father, Fred Davis, an assistant lightkeeper, was taking the principal lightkeeper, Jeff Wyatt, on horse and sleigh to L'Anse au Loup to board the coastal boat. Wyatt was taking a few days leave to visit friends and relatives in Newfoundland. After the two senior lightkeepers left, assistant keeper Jim O'Dell had trouble operating the oil light in the tower. He filled the oil tank to overflowing but apparently couldn't open the valve on an adjoining air tank to pump the fuel to the wick in the top of the lamp. Not anticipating trouble with the air tank, Jim was still holding the burning torch he used to start the main light. While fumbling with the valve with one hand, he somehow dropped the torch on the floor. Within seconds, fuel that had spilled on the floor from the overfilled tank was blazing.

Fred Davis was rounding the point in L'Anse Amour when he saw smoke billowing out from the windows on all sides of the light tower. Rushing to the station, he formed a bucket brigade from the residence to the lighthouse. Fred's seventeen-year-old son Hollis was obviously in the best physical condition to run the stairs with the buckets. "My brother ran up those 120 odd stairs thirty times with two buckets full of water each time," Bobby says, smiling broadly at the thought of his late brother's heroics.

Thanks to the efforts of Hollis Davis, the damage to the lighthouse was not great. "In fact, the worst of it was the smoke build-up on the windows and on the lens of the lamp," Bobby says. "We had to work for days and days, scrubbing and washing the sticky black stuff off the windows, but the main thing is that nobody was hurt."

An Archaeologist's Dream

History buffs are especially blessed when they visit Point Amour. Just around the corner from the lighthouse, there is an archaeological site that instantly stretches the imagination. It is the grave of a young Maritime Archaic Indian boy who died there almost eight thousand years ago. Perhaps the oldest aboriginal burial site found in North America, the grave was discovered by Memorial University archaeologists Jim Tuck and Robert McGhee in 1973. Tuck and McGhee searched the area thinking that the sandy beach in what is now L'Anse Amour would have been an ideal location for the Maritime Archaic Indians to set up camp in their pursuit of harp seals in winter and spring. Digging through five feet of stone and sand, they eventually found the skeleton of a boy approximately fourteen years of age.

As it turned out, the skeleton was far more exciting than Tuck and McGhee first thought. It didn't take the two archaeologists long to figure out that they had discovered what was possibly the oldest known gravesite on the continent. Adding to the significance of the discovery, there seemed to be something very special about the boy who had been buried there. Lying face down, he was buried with a flat rock across his back. His body had been anointed with red ochre and surrounded by carefully placed objects, probably belonging to his family. The objects included a bone necklace, a whistle made from the bone of a seabird and an assortment of knives. Two fires had been lit around the body, providing Tuck and McGhee with enough carbon samples to pinpoint when the boy died.

The ceremony accompanying the boy's burial is fascinating. Bearing in mind that the burial took place 2000 years before the construction of the Egyptian pyramids, Tuck and McGhee were amazed at the attention to detail and the great pains the family and community had taken to bury the youth. In a paper entitled " An

Archaeological Sequence from the Strait of Belle Isle, Labrador," published in the *Archaeological Survey of Canada*, Tuck and McGhee wrote:

> As far as we know at present, no peoples on earth were taking such pains in disposing of their dead in this manner at that time.

The burial site has been returned to its original state and is marked by a modest plaque briefly outlining the significance of the grave.

Wrecker's Paradise

As fascinating as an ancient burial site is, Point Amour is still best known for more recent death. The infamous "straits currents" have caused the ruin of hundreds of boats and ships of all makes and sizes. Even today, people from the Labrador Straits area talk about the loss of ships on the reefs near the lighthouse, but mostly they talk about the salvage operations of those ships by local residents.

Because of the shallow water that barely covers the dozens of rocky shoals off Point Amour, most large ships that ran aground there didn't sink below the surface. Although the rocks often ripped huge holes in a ship's bottom, causing a total loss, the vessel settled to rest between shoals with most of the hull above water. Whenever that happened, men from a dozen communities on both sides of the Straits set out in their small boats to see what they could get from the stricken vessels. They were called "wreckers."

Behaving much like scavengers, wreckers were quick to load their fishing boats with everything from rum and whisky to brass lamps from the ill-fated ships. Sometimes a shipwreck was considered heaven-sent. Even now, old timers recall stories their parents and grandparents told about ships that came ashore at the perfect time. Some stories tell of ships that were wrecked when the fishery had failed and food was scarce. Groceries salvaged from the grounded ships made the difference between a hungry winter and a bounty of supplies.

Nothing was wasted in a wrecking operation. Even items like flour that had been soaked were taken. The men would wait until the wet flour on the outside dried into a crust, then cut off the hard part with knives and salvage the dry powdered flour from inside the sacks. One lightkeeper remembers a stranded ship that provided an interesting sideshow. It seems that dozens of flour sacks floated into the bottom of the ship's stack and each time a wave washed through the hull, the pressure from the water sent flour flying up through the stack. "It was just like real heavy snow flurries comin' out of her stack every time a wave struck her," he laughs. Other stories tell of wrecked cargo ships carrying lumber that provided more than a few men with enough supplies to build extensions to their houses or construct brand new supply sheds and barns in backyards. Shipwrecks near Point Amour were a classic example of the old adage that "it's an ill wind that blows no good."

The "good" coming from the ill-fated wrecks has been the centre of controversy on more than one occasion. There were suspicions that people were benefitting so much from them that they would even pray to God for a wreck. Other stories suggest some people couldn't wait for God to respond. It is said that some residents devised a system to cause ships to go aground. According to those yarns, on stormy nights men would set up false lights on several headlands near Point Amour. The idea was to mislead ship's officers into thinking they were seeing the Point Amour lighthouse and to change their course accordingly. The altered course was thought to cause the ship to go aground.

There is no proof of such incidents, and most people are quick to point out that if false lights were erected anywhere on the coast, they would have the opposite effect. They say ships would alter course away from land instead of going further toward the shore.

Besides false lights, supernatural forces have been listed as reasons why ships ran aground. Some ships, like people, were believed destined for destruction when their time had come. Disasters, therefore, could be interpreted as acts of God. Such beliefs were widespread, according to writings by Newfoundland Judge Daniel Prowse:

Seafaring people looked upon wrecks as their lawful prizes, gifts sent to them direct by Providence, and their views about these fatalities were characteristic. The belief that Destiny, Fate, Providence or God played an active role in marine disasters, was consistent with the widespread belief among coastal residents in various supernatural phenomena, such as ghosts and ghost ships

As recently as the 1960s, some elderly Southern Shore fishermen reported seeing the lights of the long-lost ship *Southern Cross* as an omen of approaching storms. The *Southern Cross* was a sealing ship lost in March, 1914. The crew of 173 sealers, mostly young men from Conception Bay, went down with the ship, making it the worst sealing disaster in Newfoundland history. The *Southern Cross* was lost near Cape Pine on the southern shore of the Avalon Peninsula where there are many tales of wreckers and wrecking. Like the stories from Point Amour, the Cape Pine stories often allude to the belief that men positioned lights on headlands near the cape to create confusion and cause shipping disasters. A story from Cape Race tells of a ship deliberately grounded one stormy night. According to the yarn, all the ship's crew made it to shore where they were taken to a private home for the night. An old lady in the house put her arms around the captain's neck saying, "Thank God for this happy blessing in bringing your ship to the land — now we have a stock of grub for the winter; the lights on the cow's horns paid off."

Because some people believed that ships were deliberately grounded, wreckers earned a bad reputation . They were often referred to as hard-hearted; some went as far as to call them pirates. When one ship ran aground near Cape Pine in the late 1800s, the captain was so suspicious of wreckers that he refused assistance from a nearby fishing crew who offered to take the crew onboard their vessel. According to local storytellers, the captain was very rude to the fishermen. Certain they were only interested in taking the crew off the ship in order to plunder supplies, he cursed his would-be rescuers and drove them away. Risking going down in his grounded boat, the captain opted to wait for a government vessel before abandoning ship. Wherever wreckers developed a nasty reputation, some captains of ships that were stricken but not a total loss chose to refuse local rescue help and wait for official assistance.

Stories of false lights along with other natural and supernatural phenomena were so rampant that even the famous Dr. Wilfred Grenfell got involved in the controversy. In a letter to the Lloyds of London marine insurance company, quoted by author David Whalen, Sir Wilfred made what appears to be a tongue-in-cheek comment. He wrote:

> Our fishermen never pray for ships to be wrecked. There is some little doubt amongst those of us who own boats as to whether such a prayer might not prove a boomerang. However, I have known sincerely religious men to pray that, if there was going to be such a shipwreck, at least it might as well be in our neighbourhood.

Dr. Grenfell's mention of a boomerang effect refers to the high price sometimes paid for the benefits of wrecking. Several men drowned during wrecking expeditions. And in one instance, a family in Pinware on the Labrador coast lost a four-year-old daughter to what is believed to be a case of lead poisoning caused by food obtained from a 1942 shipwreck. But the benefits derived from shipwrecks far outweighed the risks, and residents of the area became so adept at the art of salvaging they were always ready to spring into action, armed with a variety of tools designed for an extremely efficient clean-up operation.

Ironically, the Grenfell Mission in Forteau, built by Sir Wilfred, was not beyond accepting some of the bounty from shipwrecks. The Forteau mission building proudly displayed a stove, an ornamental fireplace, a chest of drawers, a cupboard and a leather chair from the *Raleigh,* a British Navy ship that ran aground on Point Amour in 1922.

There are countless stories about ships that foundered near Point Amour. The biggest ship that ended her days on the jagged reefs was the 12,000-ton *SS Mariposa* in 1895. The huge vessel, heavily laden with cargo, ripped holes in the hull as far back as amidships when she struck the rocks. As the *Mariposa* started to settle stern-first in the shoal waters, its bow was elevated several stories above the surface. Although it was a calm night when the vessel struck the rocks, gale-force winds had developed by the time rescue operations started at daylight. Plans to take the sixty-six passengers to shore in lifeboats were scuttled when increasingly high winds and heavy seas made it impossible for small boats to avoid hitting the rocks.

The crew managed to get a line to land and rigged a "breeches buoy," a canvas hammock-like chair supported by ropes, also known as a bosun's (boatswain's) chair. For the passengers, it must have been daunting to climb to the ship's bow and realize the only way to safety was across a 600-foot chasm of raging white water. Author David Whalen described the scene in his book *Just one Interloper after Another*:

> One by one the corseted Victorian ladies had to shed their stately reserve and allow themselves to be lashed into the fragile-looking, uncomfortable swinging seat of the breeches buoy, before being slowly pulled across the long gap between ship and beach. As they swayed shoreward on the line, forty feet above the hissing surf, several, overcome by the frightening experience, became hysterical and were unconscious when the buoy reached safety.

Not much is known about the first few years of operation at the Point Amour lighthouse. However, Thomas Wyatt kept good records from the start of his job at the light in 1880. Thomas and his son, Jeff Wyatt, were responsible for the lighthouse for eighty years, until Jeff retired in 1961.

Thomas Wyatt was considered an eccentric by some. Other than his keen interest in collecting artifacts found on his walks around Point Amour's sandy beaches, the lightkeeper was also known as a bit of an inventor. He spent many hours in his workshop at the lightstation, testing his ideas while he worked with wood, metals and any other materials he could find.

It was not surprising, then, that Thomas Wyatt's ingenuity and quick thinking was credited with saving four men from certain death in the late 1880s. The four were crewmembers of the HMS *Lily* that ran aground on Point Amour in the fall of 1889.

On September 16, the British gunboat was riding out heavy seas in a thick fog just off the coast from Point Amour. Captain Gerald Russell heard the fog whistle from the lighthouse but thinking the sound was at least a mile away, he saw no reason to alter course. A few minutes later the *Lily* struck a reef just below the lighthouse.

The 720-ton ship struck with such force that sailors were thrown from the riggings. A huge gash was torn in the hull and the *Lily* started sinking immediately. Several lifeboats were launched and most of the crew managed to get off the ship before the vessel sank. Seven men drowned when one lifeboat swamped; however most of the men managed to swim to shore. Twenty-five men in a second lifeboat decided to stay away from the foaming water near the beach and rode out the seas in calmer waters offshore. They made it to safety the next morning.

When daylight broke, lightkeeper Thomas Wyatt could only see the masts of the British warship. By then the *Lily* had suffered such a pounding from the night's seas, she had sunk to the bottom with only the tops of her masts remaining above water. But what the lightkeeper didn't expect to see were four men clinging to the top of one mast. Thomas Wyatt knew exactly what to do. After getting a line to the men, the lightkeeper quickly rigged a canvas seat from material he found in his workshop. Amazingly, the four men were safely brought to shore one by one in the makeshift bosun's chair.

The British Admiralty officially recognized Thomas Wyatt for his actions. The Lord Commissioner of the Admiralty awarded the lightkeeper a mantle clock as a gift.

Thomas Wyatt may have witnessed more wrecks than his son did, but the younger Wyatt was on hand for the most famous ship ever to end her days off Point Amour. Just three years after he took over as principal lightkeeper from his father in 1919, Jeff Wyatt was on duty when the flagship of the British North American Squadron ran ashore on a calm day in August, 1922.

The 600-foot *Raleigh* was on a courtesy tour of American and Canadian ports that summer. In early August, it visited the west cast of Newfoundland. During that visit, Captain Bromley heard about the splendid salmon fishing in Forteau River, Labrador near Point Amour. Thinking it was time for a little rest and relaxation from the mundane chores of official visits, the captain decided he'd anchor the big ship in Forteau Bay and go ashore in a launch and check it out for himself.

Although it was a foggy afternoon, there was hardly any wind as the *Raleigh* approached the Strait of Belle Isle. There are contradictory reports of what happened next. One story claims the big navy ship altered course to avoid an iceberg and wound up on the rocks while some local accounts of the incident claim there were no icebergs in the Straits that summer. Wilfred Davis from L'Anse Amour remembers the day the *Raleigh* grounded. He disputes the iceberg argument. "The only ice Captain Bromley saw that day was in his tumbler of rum," he says with a scornful grin.

While the argument continues about the presence of icebergs, there is one indisputable fact: at 4:00 p.m. on August 8, 1922, the sleek hull of the *Raleigh* was ripped down more than half its length on the jagged rocks, almost directly in front of the Point Amour lighthouse. The great weight of the navy ship carried her huge bulk crashing in over the same rocks that had claimed the *Lily* in 1889.

Astounded at the grounding, Captain Bromley ordered a lifeboat over the side to get a line ashore immediately. Although there were no significant seas at the time, something went wrong. It appears some young sailors panicked and their small overloaded motorboat capsized before they could reach the beach, 600 feet away. Eleven men were drowned. Fortunately for the rest of the crew, one of the sailors did manage to get ashore with a line from the ship. Jeff Wyatt and several other lightkeepers were waiting on the beach to haul the man to safety and secure the rope to a large rock. Rescue operations began immediately. One after the other, all 650 men climbed hand over hand on the rope to the shoreline.

Jeff Wyatt had seen his father deal with dozens of shipwrecked crews but he could never have been prepared for the task of accommodating nearly 700 people at once in a lighthouse. But, like his father, Jeff Wyatt proved to be a resourceful man and found shelter

Courtesy Canadian Coast Guard, Fisheries and Oceans

Point Amour lighthouse and fog alarm building

for many of the men in the lighthouse buildings. They slept in sheds and workshops. Even the lighthouse itself was full of men all the way up the tower, 120 feet above ground. He took the remaining crew to homes in nearby communities. They were a little cramped for space but the men were well cared for. Five days later, the Canadian liner *Montrose* arrived in Forteau Bay from Montreal and took the ship's crew back to England. The bodies of the eleven crewmembers were buried near the lighthouse. Their graves are still identified today.

The wreck of the *Raleigh* provided a bonanza for wreckers. Dozens of small boats from all along the Straits converged on the area to take anything of value. One of the most prized items shared by wreckers was a cache of forty-gallon kegs of fine West Indian rum. Some residents in the area still remember the "fine Christmas they had that year." In fact, one community did so well from salvaging the wreck they renamed their community Raleigh.

While local people enjoyed every minute of the salvaging operations, the British Admiralty was terribly embarrassed by the grounding. The *Raleigh* became a major attraction for international shipping crews. It is said that some, especially officers on American navy ships, made a point of dropping by to look at the wreck of the warship, then recounted their visit to the British with smirks and mocking detail. The British Admiralty became so humiliated they decided to blow up the *Raleigh* with tons of explosives in 1926.

While the British investigated the cause of the sinking, the debate over whether there were icebergs in the Strait that summer continued. Jeff Wyatt was asked if there were icebergs in the Strait on August 8, 1922. Not wanting to cause trouble for the captain or the ship's officers, the young lightkeeper responded diplomatically. "If Captain Bromley says he altered course to avoid an iceberg, then I guess he saw an iceberg — it was a foggy day and I couldn't see far from shore." The combination of fog and icebergs and the infamous Strait currents have taken their toll on more ships than anyone can recall. But the long list of wrecks would probably have doubled or even tripled had it not been for the tall lighthouse that is still a major aid to navigation for international shipping and local fishing vessels in the Straits.

Chapter Six

The French Connection

Green Island

Lighthouse keepers in Newfoundland and Labrador are constantly on the lookout for vessels in trouble, especially in stormy winter weather. Usually they expect to see commercial fishing vessels or, depending on the location, large ocean-going ships. In some northern locations, the requirement of lightkeepers to be on constant lookout is not as great in winter because shipping is practically closed, shut out by heavy arctic ice that chokes the main waterways. Lightkeepers on Newfoundland's south coast don't have the luxury of slow traffic months. Marine activity there is nearly as heavy in winter as it is in summer, even by small open boats. This is especially true in the vicinity of Green Island, Fortune Bay.

Located six miles southwest of Point May on the Burin Peninsula, the one-mile-long island is almost exactly halfway between the coast of Newfoundland and the French island of St. Pierre. Even today, small-boat fishermen are often in contact with the lightstation, keeping the lightkeepers informed of their whereabouts and activities in case one of the infamous south-coast thick-as-pea-soup fogs rolls in over them. Often, fishermen in small open speedboats call to get the latest weather conditions and forecast updates.

A Winter's Tale

Besides being a favourite fishing area for small, near-shore vessels, the waters around Green Island have always been popular with seabird hunters from St. Pierre and Miquelon and Newfoundland. Lightkeepers on Green Island have often been uncertain what country many of the boats were from.

Courtesy Canadian Coast Guard, Fisheries and Oceans

Green Island

Veteran lightkeepers Murdock Stewart, Ambrose Price, George Mavin, Eric Kendell and others can relate many stories about incidents when French boaters ran into trouble and came ashore to stay at the lightstation until conditions improved or until someone came to take them back home. Not all the French hunters made it to the safety and comfort of the lighthouse.

On a cold but clear January morning in 1992, lightkeepers Ron Thornhill and Gord Price, both from Fortune, got up extra early to check the weather. With just one look out the window from the lighthouse residence on Green Island, the two men knew from experience that it was going to be an ideal morning to get a couple of saltwater ducks for dinner. At the breakfast table they discussed their hunting strategy as they had done many times before.

By dawn the pair were headed for Western Point, the end of the island facing St. Pierre. Just as they reached the Point, both Gord and Ron heard a voice calling from the rocks surrounding Little Green

Island, a small rocky enclave less than a half-mile southwest of Green Island. At first, neither lightkeeper thought anything about the voice. Both men figured they were hearing the chatter of other enthusiastic early morning hunters. Even when they got close enough to see a man on Little Green, they saw nothing that immediately made them think anything was amiss. But it wasn't long before the experienced outdoorsmen wondered about what they had seen and heard. "I said to Gord, several times, that it was strange that fellow was up so high on the rock from the water if they were duck hunting," Ron says. Normally hunters stay closer to the water. Hunters don't usually make that much noise either, he thought.

Becoming more and more perplexed, Ron decided to take another look, this time from a better vantage point. Climbing to a grassy area up high on Western Point, Ron could now see three people. Two were standing on the rocks near the water's edge. The third person, the one they had seen earlier, was standing on top of a twenty-foot high rock waving his arms and shouting. With the westerly breeze carrying the sound of the man's voice across the water, Ron heard the man shout "Help!" Calling to Gord that something must be wrong, Ron said they'd better get over to Little Green as fast as they could. After a brisk walk back to the east side of Green Island, the lightkeepers launched their dory to investigate.

The combined forces of wind and tides coming against them meant it was slow going for Ron and Gord but they made steady time. When they were about ten minutes away from the rocks, Gord noticed something strange. There was something floating in the water near the rocks where the people were standing. "It looks like it might be a boat, but it's awfully low in the water," Gord said to Ron, peering intently at the dark grey object. He was right. A few minutes later, they could clearly see it was indeed a boat but it was bottom up and nearly completely submerged. As they drew closer to the three people on the rocks, Ron was surprised to recognize one of the two adults as an acquaintance of his from St. Pierre. "His name was Jean. I don't know his last name but I remembered him being in Fortune a lot — I think he had a girlfriend there or something." Moments later,

Boat slipway on Green Island — the boat on the left was used by lightkeepers Ron Thornhill and Gord Price in the rescue of three St. Pierre residents in 1992.

the lightkeepers noticed that one of the three was a young boy, about eight or nine years old.

Although the three were French-speaking, they spoke English well enough to communicate their story. "There were four of us," they said, as they began to tell what had happened. When the owner and operator of the twenty-three-foot boat attempted to land on the rocky coastline, he rode the crest of a wave up as high as he could on a smooth slanting rock. The idea was to have the bow of the boat come to rest on the rock when the wave receded. That way, the three in the front could jump from the boat safely onto the rock.

It seems he miscalculated the height of the seas or the angle of the rock, or he rode in on a wave that was bigger than the other ones. When the wave receded, the entire length of the boat was high and dry. With no water underneath to buoy the small aluminum vessel, it toppled over on one side. Before anyone could jump, another large wave rushed in, flipping the boat upside down and dragging it back into the ocean. The two men and the boy in the bow section were thrown overboard, but luckily they were swept back close to the rocks on a wave and managed to climb to safety onshore. Sadly, the owner was standing inside the small wheelhouse at the stern and couldn't get out of the submerged boat when it flipped.

Although soaked to the bone, the three survivors appeared in reasonably good condition, despite sub-zero temperatures. The boy had lost his boots while struggling to climb from the water to the rocks and the only thing keeping his feet from frostbite was a pair of woollen mittens one of the men had given him to haul on over his toes.

Although they were extremely uncomfortable, the men refused the lightkeepers' offer to come to the lighthouse where they could change into dry clothes. Instead, they asked if Ron and Gord would search the waters around the island to see if they could find their missing friend.

Although the two lightkeepers were concerned about the three becoming hypothermic, they understood their anxiety and agreed to the search. They circled the small island several times but found nothing. Aware that nearly two hours had passed since the accident, the lightkeepers knew that chances of finding the man alive in the frigid Atlantic Ocean ranged from slim to nil, so once again they turned their attention to the survivors.

As the two men and the boy huddled shivering on the rocks, Ron and Gord again appealed to them to come to the lighthouse. "At least, let us bring the boy with us," they asked. Again the three expressed their gratitude but this time they refused because another small open boat from St. Pierre had appeared not far offshore from Green Island. Grateful for the offers of assistance, the three preferred to be with their fellow countrymen if they could. Although miserably cold and uncomfortable, especially without boots, the young boy declined the offer. "I think he was afraid to be separated from the two adults, especially since one of them was his uncle," Ron says.

Satisfied that the two St. Pierre bird hunters onboard the boat offshore had seen them and were steaming toward the survivors, Gord and Ron decided to go back to the lighthouse. Noting that the approaching boat was a small open speedboat with no facilities to

Courtesy Ron Thornhill

Little Green Island — site of the drowning of a St. Pierre bird hunter in January, 1992

provide warmth for the three, the lightkeepers said they would be back as soon as possible with warm, dry clothing.

Once back at the lightstation, Gord hurried to find all the clothes, boots and blankets they could spare while Ron notified Coast Guard Radio in St. Lawrence of the accident.

It was just after 10:30 a.m. when Gord and Ron arrived back near the rocks of Little Green Island. By then, the scene had changed considerably. Word had reached St. Pierre about the accident via VHF radio, and several high-powered speedboats from the French island had already raced to the site. There were also two larger vessels on the way.

With spirits lifted by the arrival of their friends, the three survivors, although chilled to the bone and losing strength, were overjoyed to see Ron and Gord approach with a bundle of warm, dry clothing and blankets. Quickly shedding their soaked and nearly frozen clothes, the three were soon as comfortable as possible under the circumstances.

A few minutes later, the waters between Green Island and Little Green Island resembled a city marina. Besides the lightkeepers' dory and the St. Pierre speedboats of various sizes and descriptions, two larger French vessels had arrived on the scene. Above them, a Canadian Coast Guard Search and Rescue fixed-wing aircraft from Gander was circling the little island, searching for the missing man.

As the survivors were transferred to the *Miquelon*, a yacht owned by the St. Pierre government, Ron and Gord were considering what to do next. Satisfied that they had done all they could for the survivors, they could have gone back to the lighthouse. But there was still unfinished business. Glancing up to the windows of the *Miquelon*, Ron saw the young boy staring back at him. "I'll never forget the look on his face," Ron says. "I can't describe it; it was a look of anguish, as if he was in a trance." Whether it had anything to do with the look on the boy's face is unclear, but Ron Thornhill and Gord Price both knew they couldn't leave until the missing man was found.

They didn't have long to wait. Sometime about noon, two French divers arrived on the scene. Within a few minutes they discovered the body of the fifty-six-year-old man on the ocean bottom, directly underneath his capsized boat. After assisting the divers in getting the body onboard one of the St. Pierre vessels, the lightkeepers said farewell and returned to the lighthouse.

The traumatic psychological impact of dealing with tragedy lingers. Although Coast Guard officials offered to bring the light-keepers in from the island and take back replacements to finish their twenty-eight-day shift, both Ron and Gord refused, saying they would be all right. Eventually, they were all right, but it took a while. "For the first few nights we couldn't sleep much," Ron remembers. "I'd drift off for a while but then I would suddenly wake up, sort of startled like."

As the days and nights passed, life slowly returned to normal for Ron Thornhill and Gord Price. Eventually both were back to their regular routine of lightkeeping duties. While neither man will ever forget the tragedy of the loss of one life, both have the satisfaction of knowing they saved three people from perishing on the rocks of Little Green Island that day.

The French government quickly recognized both lightkeepers with an award for their efforts.

Déjà Vu

Only two and a half years after Ron Thornhill and Gordon Price carried out a rescue mission, Green Island lightkeepers were once again called to perform a rescue. This time the lightkeepers were Brian Cull from Marystown and CalvinB Thornhill from Fortune, younger brother of Ron Thornhill.

Saturday, July 23, 1994 was a pleasant day on the south coast of Newfoundland. Winds were light and skies were clear. About six miles southwest of Green Island, the Bonnieul family from St, Pierre was up bright and early, preparing to take advantage of the fine summer weekend that was shaping up. The plan was to travel to their summer cottage just a few kilometres north of St. Pierre in Langlade on the southern end of Miquelon Island. After packing their weekend supplies, the family went to their speedboat in St. Pierre harbour.

On such a nice summer day, the twenty-minute boat trip to the cottage was going to be one of the highlights of the outing. That was especially true for the Bonnieul children, ten-year-old Xandier and his six-year-old sister, Jennifer. Vicki Cormier, a ten-year-old cousin of the Bonnieul children, was also along for the weekend trip to the country.

Because it was a nice warm day, Jean Claude Bonnieul decided to give the family a little extra boating fun before heading to the cottage.

About two o'clock in the afternoon, just as they approached Langlade, winds blowing off the land suddenly increased and white-caps developed. Before Jean Claude could reduce the engine's power, a large wave struck the boat broadside, nearly filling the small vessel with water. Unable to turn the water-laden boat to face into the wind in an attempt to ride the waves, there was nothing the family could do but hope for the best. But best hopes quickly faded as another wave struck, again from the broadside. This time, the boat capsized, throwing all five people into the ocean. Four of the five managed to swim and tread water until they could climb onto the bottom of the overturned boat. But six-year old Jennifer Bonnieul was nowhere to be seen. It took a few moments before they realized the young girl was trapped underneath the overturned vessel.

After two attempts diving into the ocean, the little girl's father finally managed to get her from the water and on top of the over-turned boat with the rest of family. But the ordeal took a heavy toll on Jennifer. She'd inhaled large amounts of water during the time she was under the boat. With no one nearby to help them, the only thing the two adults and three children could do was huddle together on the keel of the boat and pray that someone would see them soon.

Sadly, no one did see them that day. All afternoon the five bobbed around the ocean on the overturned boat as wave after wave washed over them. Although they were quickly drifting away from the French islands toward Green Island in Fortune Bay, the family remained in good spirits for most of the day. As long as there was daylight there was hope of being sighted by passing boats. With warmth from the July sunshine, they knew they could stave off hypothermia for several hours. Surely someone would spot them before dark, they thought.

Although the ocean between Green Island and St. Pierre was busy with marine traffic, no one saw the overturned boat that afternoon. Four and five-foot waves hid the victims from the view of even nearby vessels, and brisk winds carried their shouts for help in the wrong direction.

By evening the five were growing weary. When a thick fog rolled in just before sunset, the air grew cold and damp, and spirits grew dim. All night the family huddled on the small overturned boat as Jean Claude Bonnieul cradled his daughter in his arms, watching helplessly as she drifted in and out of consciousness.

On Green Island, Saturday was a routine day for Brian Cull and Calvin Thornhill. There was the usual summer boating activity around the island but nothing out of the ordinary—with one excep-tion. Around suppertime that evening, the lightkeepers noticed a fishing vessel from St. Pierre steaming unusually close to the island.

Both men acknowledged that it was strange for a longliner to come so close to the cliffs but other than that, the two thought nothing more about it. They had no way of knowing the people on the vessel were already searching for the missing family.

As daylight faded, a misty grey blanket of fog settled over the one-kilometre-long island, reducing visibility to almost zero. Although Brian and Calvin couldn't see anything, they could still hear the sound of boats passing the island from time to time that night. There was nothing unusual about continuous boating traffic on summer nights so they still had no reason to think that anything was wrong.

As the thick layer of fog continued to shroud Fortune Bay the next morning, Brian was busy cooking Sunday dinner while Calvin puttered around, doing other lightkeeping duties. At 12.20 p.m., just as dinner was ready, they received a call from the Coast Guard Radio Station in St. Lawrence alerting them that a family from St. Pierre were long overdue on a boating trip. A party of five people had left St. Pierre around noon on Saturday in a small open boat and hadn't been seen since.

Aware that twenty-four hours in an open boat could severely weaken people, especially in damp foggy weather, both men wasted no time in starting their search. While Brian put dinner on hold, Calvin grabbed a gun from the rack to use to send a signal if they saw anything unusual. Within minutes, both lightkeepers were on their way to the western corner of the island facing St. Pierre.

As they walked toward the edge of the cliffs, Calvin and Brian silently observed wind and weather conditions in case they needed to launch their boat. "Unlike the day before, Sunday's weather would discourage anyone from going out on a boat ride for pleasure," Brian recalls. Besides the discomfort of the heavy fog, seas were getting rough and winds were brisk.

Visibility was restricted to a few hundred feet so Calvin fired a shot, hoping that if anyone was in trouble nearby they would respond. Neither Calvin nor Brian was surprised when there was no reply. "To be honest, we figured that if anyone out of St. Pierre was drifting in the direction of winds and tides for the last twenty hours or more, they were probably up in the other end of Fortune Bay by now," says Brian.

Not prepared to give up looking after firing just one shot and having one walk about, Calvin and Brian walked to Northwest Head and fired another shot. There was still no response so they headed for the southwest end of the island. That's when a miracle happened. Just as the two lightkeepers reached the edge of the island, the dense fog parted in front of them for a few moments. At first it cleared just long enough for Calvin and Brian to see four orange life jackets about 300 feet from shore. Calvin fired another shot, and to their surprise they heard at least two voices calling back to them. Peering through the fog, Brian and Calvin could see what appeared to be four people drifting in an open boat.

At first it seemed that everyone was in good shape, according to Brian. "Although we couldn't see much of the boat, there was a swell on at the time and everything appeared normal, it just seemed like the boat was hidden from our view by the swell so we figured everyone was dry and everything you know — that they were fine."

Thinking the family were not in any immediate danger, Brian decided to go to the lightstation and get a life ring, hoping the people could row the boat close enough to shore to throw the ring to them. While Brian was gone, Calvin, an experienced boat operator, thought it would be best if he went out in the dory to see if he could lend a hand. By the time Brian returned, Calvin had already launched the boat and was on his way around the island, headed toward the family. Brian ran along the edge of the island, keeping vigil on both his fellow lightkeeper and the people offshore, making sure Calvin knew where to find them in the fog.

It was not until he was a few feet away from the Bonneiul family that Calvin noticed there were five people instead of four and that instead of sitting in an upright vessel, they were all huddled on the keel of a submerged boat. What Calvin thought was going to be a simple matter of handing someone a set of oars or, at worst, towing a small boat with engine trouble, suddenly turned into a very technical rescue mission, requiring acute skills.

Not knowing the physical or emotional conditions of the victims,

Calvin's first concern was to approach them carefully. Winds were brisk and seas were choppy. Calvin knew that if anyone panicked and rushed he could easily be dealing with two overturned boats.

Calvin's many years of boating experience paid off. Positioning the dory on the windward side of the stricken boat, he used the wind as an instrument to keep both boats from drifting apart. That way, the people could make a more comfortable exit from the slippery bottom of the overturned boat into his dory.

His next problem was dealing with the frightened children. Somewhat delirious after spending a long night huddled on the keel of a small boat in the cold Atlantic Ocean, the two older children were afraid to move — afraid to let go of the tiny bit of security they had become accustomed to for nearly twenty-four hours.

With a little coaxing and reassurance from Calvin, they finally mustered the energy and nerve to leave their perch. With Calvin's help, Bridgett Bonnieul, her son and her niece were safely in the dory within minutes. The father, still carrying his unconscious six-year-old daughter, was the last to get onboard.

Back on Green Island, Brian watched the rescue operation unfold, still unaware that they were dealing with people who had spent the night on a swamped boat. Constantly keeping his eyes trained on the dory as Calvin steamed around the island to the landing point in the cove, Brian was on the beach to meet them when they came ashore.

Although numbed from the cold water and the chilly six-degree air temperature, the adults and two children were in remarkably good condition and stepped from the dory to the boat landing without assistance.

The twenty-four-year-old lightkeeper from Marystown noticed the swollen hands and pale colouring of the adults and two children, but Brian Cull was totally unprepared for what happened next. He hadn't seen the young girl until Calvin took her in his arms to pass her to him. "I can't explain what I felt when I first looked at her," Brian remembers. "I felt like I froze solid but I remember my arms reaching to take her from Calvin but there was something about her eyes — I can't explain it; her eyes were big but lifeless and without any sign of dilation."

Brian Cull can't remember his exact feelings during the next few moments. He experienced a mixture of a million fleeting thoughts and emotions all at once. Although he recognized that there were no apparent vital signs, he thought it might be possible that the girl was still alive. The only thing he knew for sure was that he had to try and save her in case there was hope.

With adrenaline pumping through every vein in his body, Brian took the girl in his arms and ran toward the lighthouse. Although he thought it was crucial to get the child to the warmth of the residence as soon as possible, Brian paused for a few moments along the trail to give her mouth-to-mouth resuscitation. When there was no apparent sign of improvement in the girl's condition, Brian picked her up and continued to run to the house. Once inside the residence, the lightkeeper removed the life jacket from the young girl, loosened her shirt, wrapped her in a blanket and administered CPR.

A few minutes later, when Cal arrived with the Bonnieul family, Brian was still giving the young girl mouth-to-mouth resuscitation. Aware that Calvin was taking care of the family, getting them dry clothes and making them tea and lunch, the younger lightkeeper became obsessed with saving Jennifer. "I kept thinking that, supposing there was a glimmer of life there and that I would be told by some doctor later that she died while under my care—I could never live with myself, so I had to do everything humanly possible to try and save her."

Brian Cull tried everything he could do that day. Although satisfied that he was properly administering CPR, he wondered if there was anything else he could try. There wasn't. A quick phone call to a doctor at the Health Sciences Centre in St. John's confirmed that the only thing to do was to continue administering mouth-to-mouth resuscitation for another few minutes.

Although there was no sign of a pulse and no dilation of her pupils, Brian continued to perform CPR more feverishly than ever on the child. After what seemed an eternity to him, but what in fact was about twenty minutes, he reluctantly accepted the inevitable.

Drained, physically and emotionally, Brian finally gave up the struggle. Feeling as if he was walking on feet of lead, he walked outdoors and sat down, savouring every breath of fresh air going into his lungs. A few moments later Calvin joined him and asked if he was prepared to accept that there was no hope of saving Jennifer. "By then I was shaking, feeling as if my nerves were coming unravelled, but I said 'yes,' I knew she was gone," Brian says.

Calvin then asked if Brian wanted him to tell the family that there was nothing more that could be done for their daughter. After all his intense efforts to save her, Brian felt a sense of bonding and posses-siveness about Jennifer and felt strongly that he should be the one to talk to her family.

Aware that it was not within a lightkeeper's authority to pro-nounce anyone dead, Brian waited a few moments to recoup, before finally mustering enough courage to go back inside the house to see the family.

Driven more by intuition than rational thought, he went to Bridgett Bonnieul first. "I didn't know what to say to the poor woman, so I just put it as simply as I could. 'My love,' I said, 'I think your little girl is gone — I can't do any more for her.'"

For the second time that afternoon Brian Cull was overwhelmed with grief. "Some people would say I cracked, but I wouldn't agree with that; however, I was so totally overcome with emotion that I could hardly function," Brian admits.

Meanwhile, Calvin was busy taking care of the business at hand. He was in constant communication with both Canadian and French authorities. Between phone calls, Calvin did a splendid job of keep-ing the four survivors occupied and informed of everything that was happening. While they waited for a Coast Guard Search and Rescue (SAR) helicopter to arrive, Calvin made sure the survivors were as warm and comfortable as possible, feeding them tea and snacks.

It wasn't long before Calvin had help dealing with the family. Word of the rescue spread rapidly. By 2:30, approximately a dozen speedboats from St. Pierre had landed in a small cove on Green Island. Among the people on board were friends and relatives of the Bonneiul family who had come to try and comfort them.

One of the boats brought a doctor from St. Pierre. Desperate to know if he had failed to save Jennifer, the first thing Brian wanted to know was whether the doctor could estimate the time of death. "I just had to know if I gave up too soon — I just had to know," Brian recalls. Although the French/English language barrier was an impediment, Brian managed to make the doctor understand his question and, more importantly, the reason for it. The young lightkeeper was deeply troubled with the doctor's response. Acknowledging that he couldn't be precise about the time of death, the doctor estimated that Jennifer had been dead for at least an hour. Realizing that he had tried to revive Jennifer for more than an hour, Brian was painfully disheartened. Later he was relieved to learn that the doctor meant the girl had died at least an hour before the lightkeepers found the family, and not an hour before Brian made the inquiry.

With nothing more to do but wait for a Canadian Coast Guard helicopter to come and take the family to St. Pierre, the two light-keepers spent their time chatting with the French visitors. When the large Labrador helicopter landed, the crowd grew quiet as the medic and pilot walked inside the residence.

Both Calvin Thornhill and Brian Cull have vivid memories of that precise moment. Although the Search and Rescue pilot was trained to deal with casualties, the sight of the lifeless Jennifer Bonneiul was too much for even him. "I guess it was because it was a beautiful young girl lying there," Brian recalls thinking. But whatever his thoughts, as he removed his helmet, the helicopter pilot took one look at the body, turned and, with tears in his eyes, walked outside for a few moments to regain his composure.

A few minutes later, Jean Claude and Bridgett Bonneiul, their son and niece and the body of their daughter Jennifer were airlifted by helicopter back home.

On Green Island, Calvin Thornhill and Brian Cull were left alone to ponder the day's events. Things would not be normal for a long time. Brian left the island the next day and requested a change of workstations. After working at the lighthouse on Little Burin Island for three years, he finally went back to Green Island in 1998.

Calvin Thornhill completed his shift on the island that month.

Green Island — the French island of St. Pierre is on the left and Langlade is on the right.

Today, he smiles when he remembers the day after the rescue. Someone thought it would be therapeutic for Calvin to have a family member visit him after the ordeal. It was supposed to be a surprise, but somehow Calvin had more than a sneaky suspicion that his son was onboard the boat from Fortune that landed on the island the next morning. "Surprised or not, I was sure glad to see him — it was like medicine."

Chapter Seven

The Forans of Point Latine

Latine? La Tine? Lat Nee?

No one knows what it means. In fact no one knows if it is, or ever was, an actual word. Some think it might be a derivative from a French, Latin or Italian word. There is a headland near Argentia called Point Latine, but no one is sure how it got the name. Some old-timers claim that a foreign ship called *Latine* went aground there many years ago, hence the name Point Latine.

No one is even quite sure of the correct pronunciation. Today, some call it "La tine" with a French-flavoured accent, but older people, especially those from the area, pronounce it "Lat nee" with the emphasis on Lat. That's the way retired Christian Brother Francis Foran pronounces it and he ought to know. He grew up in the lighthouse on Point Latine.

Archival records of the Point Latine lighthouse are practically nonexistent. The lighthouse was bulldozed into the ground in 1942 to make way for the construction of the U.S. Military Base in Argentia. The only thing remaining is the headland itself. The American bulldozers even altered the configuration of the land surrounding the lighthouse by levelling some of the small hills during construction.

Built in 1906, the lighthouse was "kept" by the Foran family until the tractors moved in to destroy it. Frank (Francis) Foran, took over as lightkeeper in 1908, two years after the light was built. He died in 1926 but his wife Caroline stayed, literally, until the last minute. The "dozers" were on the property ready to plough the lighthouse, the residence and the barn into the ground when someone issued the

Point Latine, 1921

command to "wait." Caroline Foran was not quite ready to leave. Although she had her things packed and ready to go, the sixty-one-year old woman sat in her rocking chair, staring silently out the living room window.

Caroline Foran had much to think about that morning. For thirty-six years, the lightstation was the place where she raised a family and watched them grow until most of them left Newfoundland to find work in Canada and the United States. It was the place where, for a while, she was the lighthouse keeper, perhaps the only woman in Newfoundland in the mid-1900s to ever hold that position. It was the place from where she had buried her daughter Clara. It was also the place from where she had buried her second husband, Frank.

What would become of her, she wondered? What would she do? Where would she live? Would her women friends who always visited the lighthouse on Sunday to chat and take pictures still stay in touch? Would the nurses at the Argentia hospital still need their uniforms ironed and starched? If not, how would she make enough money to live on?

As memories flowed like the ocean currents in front of her

window, Caroline's tranquillity was broken when a family friend opened the door to quietly tell her it was time to leave. "Sitting there like that, looking out the window, she reminded me of Whistler's Mother," Matt Lee said.

A few hours later, Caroline Foran's home along with the Point Latine lighthouse was razed to the ground. Within months, no one would have recognized the place where the light had proudly stood. The Americans had constructed an airplane runway that extended all the way to the edge of the lighthouse property.

Like the 477 other residents who had lost their homes during the construction of the Argentia base, life for Caroline Foran would never be the same. In his 1990 book, *A Friendly Invasion,* John N. Cardoulis quotes an unnamed U.S. naval historian who wrote about the upheaval caused by the Americans:

> After the rumours became facts, it dawned on the people that they would have to be uprooted, their homes torn down and they would have to settle elsewhere. This movement would include the (Roman Catholic) church, priest's house, school and hall, and three cemeteries.
>
> So then, began the trauma, the sorrow and frustration of moving from their homes to where they did not know.

Years later Caroline Foran's son Francis, reflecting on those years and events, wrote about his mother and her life of hardship:

> Like many of the uprooted people from Argentia, mother was never again as contented as she had been in Point Latine.

His mother's contentment during her thirty-four years there is perhaps one of the reasons Brother Francis Foran has such pleasant memories of growing up on Point Latine. Brother Foran has written about some of those memories. Because Point Latine was situated in a community and not on a remote headland or isolated island, the young son of Frances Sr. and Caroline Foran had lots of friends other than family. He says people of all ages regularly visited the lighthouse. Boys often came to sail their boats in Duck Pond, a small pond located near the lighthouse. Young Francis had a sailboat made by Bernard Power from Argentia. "It was the envy of all the other boys," he smiles. Sometimes his friends came just to talk and, according to Brother Foran, "to do a bit of boyish bragging."

Brother Foran remembers one particular day in the early 1930s when three boys from Argentia came to visit. After running out of things to do and talk about, they decided to try something new. One of them figured that it was high time they all tried smoking; after all they were young men of ten or twelve years of age.

After deciding that the roof of the barn was a safe place for their big adventure, all four climbed to the top of the building, settling on the side facing away from the lighthouse residence. The ringleader produced a plug of tobacco and some brown paper. Being much too close to home to risk the consequences of getting caught at such a wicked deed, young Frances cleverly declined the invitation. That didn't deter his three friends though. Atop the Point Latine barn was all the security they needed. There were no worries about appropriate ventilation to conceal the evidence. The continuous Point Latine winds would take care of that. Soon, crudely rolled cigarettes were produced. With machismo resembling a John Wayne swagger, someone struck a match and lit up.

"The result was disastrous," remembers the Christian Brother, laughing. "After taking a few puffs, two of the boys became extremely sick. One fellow slid off the roof and finished his first smoking escapade by falling over the fence below the barn roof."

Brother Foran's memories of his early years on Point Latine are fond recollections of a simple but satisfying life. He remembers competitive but friendly games with his friends. He remembers a slide, probably a birthday gift, made for him by his brother Ronald. "It had one-piece runners, covered with pork-barrel hoops. With a little use, the metal runners became two shining strips, giving me the fastest slide in town."

Francis Foran has many memories of Duck Pond, also called Frog Pond, although there were no frogs there. Besides racing their little sailboats in the pond, the boys spent many hours trying to catch juvenile trout known as "pricklies." The fishing gears of choice were hairnets, usually supplied by their mothers. The hairnets were often tied to the ends of sticks and strung across the top of the water, much the same as commercial saltwater fishing gillnets. To eight and nine-year-old boys, two-inch pricklies were practically the same as eight-foot swordfish.

Duck Pond was a constant source of enlightenment as well as entertainment for the Foran children. Francis Foran remembers the pond providing his first glimpses of the wonder and beauty of nature, something he wrote about in later years in a collection of personal essays:

> Sometimes, in winter, especially on stormy days, waves from the nearby ocean came crashing over the beach into the pond, increasing its size. In spring, the pond shrunk back to its original dimensions.
>
> To the ducks and geese, the pond was paradise. It also supplied us the humour of watching a mother hen with a brood of little ducks. She would run up and down the shore while the baby ducks swam serenely around the pond.
>
> When chickens or ducks were hatching, there was certain to be one that couldn't quite make it out of the egg. Mother always came to the rescue. The egg was brought into the house, a hole was pricked into the shell and the egg was wrapped in cloth. It was then placed in a container and laid on the back of the stove or in the oven with the door open. Within an hour, another baby chick or duck was waddling around.
>
> We didn't need books to explain the beginnings of life.

The young Francis Foran had more than ducks to observe. Like many other lightkeepers, the Forans kept horses, sheep and a variety of other domestic animals. When lambs were born, there was sure to be one that needed special attention from Mrs. Foran. This little animal often became a "pet" lamb after frequently being taken inside the house and fed from a bottle.

Capturing adult sheep for shearing or slaughter was always a challenge. Francis Foran and his friends herded the animals to the beach where the designated sheep would be separated from the others by chasing it to a sandy area. On the beach, the animal never had a chance at freedom. With the ocean on one side and all four legs sinking several inches in sand, it was a matter of time before the sheep tired and became an easy capture. There was no need of a sheepdog on Point Latine.

Although their primary purpose was to work, horses were also a source of pleasure. Francis Foran remembers lying on the cart on a load of hay and holding the reins as a very special privilege for a young boy. It was such a privilege he wrote a little poem about it.

> Frank Cleary drives a Motor Car
> Foley drives the Train
> Frank Foran drives a horse and Gig
> But he gets there just the same

History in the Making

Some of Brother Francis Foran's essays recount humorous anecdotes surrounding historical events. When trains first started the Argentia run, hundreds of people from communities all along the rail line came out, eager to see the so-called iron monster. At the Villa Marie stop, a Mr. Foley, the engineer, asked one of the female bystanders what she thought of the big machine. Foley, his face black from coal-dust, was a little surprised when she replied, "It's hell afloat and it's the divil drivin' it!"

Iron monsters or not, trains became commonplace as part of the rapidly changing Argentia and Point Latine townscapes when twelve thousand Americans set up quarters on the new Naval Base in the early 1940s.

Equally as common in those days were warships.

A scene from August 11, 1941 is still indelibly etched in Brother Foran's memory. Around eight o'clock that evening the sun was disappearing into the ocean just off Red Island, a large wooded island about five miles west of Argentia. Sitting on the hill overlooking the bay, Francis Foran knew something special was going on when he saw two large battleships accompanied by seventeen destroyers slip past Point Latine, heading into shimmering blue waters in the Placentia Bay sunset. Later Brother Foran wrote:

> I read about Churchill and Roosevelt meeting somewhere in the Atlantic. When I saw the picture of the *Arkansas* and *Prince of Wales*, (and *Augusta*) at anchor in front of the Issacs, I made the connection.
>
> This armada was certainly worth a picture but base security didn't encourage the use of cameras. Actually, a camera wasn't necessary — it was a sight never to be forgotten.

Francis knew there was something special about that armada, but at the time he had no idea of the significance of what he was observing. He was watching the convoy of British and U.S. navy ships carrying American President, Franklin D. Roosevelt, and England's Prime Minister, Sir Winston Churchill, along with the Chiefs of Staff and naval and military commanders from both countries. Roosevelt and Churchill sat in conference for the next three days. The Atlantic Conference was the forerunner to the signing of the Atlantic Charter, bringing the United States into World War II as an ally of Britain. The Charter was signed on August 14 on one of the warships just a short distance offshore from the Point Latine lighthouse.

There was a good reason the waters just off Argentia were chosen for the signing of the Charter. Churchill, desperate for navy destroyers in the battle against Germany, turned to the United States for assistance. Following months of negotiations, the U.S. agreed to give Britain fifty used destroyers in return for the right to lease land in various parts of the British Empire on which the U.S. could build military bases. Britain accepted the deal and offered the United States the right to lease land for a period of ninety-nine years in both Newfoundland and Bermuda.

Although the official agreement between the two governments, commonly referred to as the "destroyers-for-bases" deal, was not signed until March 27, 1941, Argentia was long-favoured by the Americans. Jutting out into the northwest Atlantic Ocean on the closest landmass to Europe, Argentia's year-round ice-free harbour had already been selected by the Americans in the fall of 1940 as the ideal site for a military base. By the end of December 1940, construction of the base had already started. Because of its excellent location, Argentia was quickly chosen to be one of the key bases for the Allied Forces in the North Atlantic during World War II. The huge U.S. military base that was subsequently established there was the most expensive of the American overseas bases built during the war. Costing over $45,000,000, it consisted of a Naval Operating Base and a Naval Air Station with three runways on the north side of Argentia Harbour. A U.S. Army Base, known as Fort McAndrew, was constructed on the south side of the harbour. The Naval Operating Base and Air Station served throughout World War II as a base for both United States and Allied forces. Following the war, the base continued to operate, but, on a constantly declining scale. In 1974 the Air Station was abandoned, and in 1975 the Naval Station was closed.

The Sea That Shook the Light

Twelve years before the Atlantic Charter was signed, a very young Francis Foran was having supper with his mother and family at the lighthouse residence when something strange happened. It was Monday, November 18, 1929. Like every other Monday evening, it was "hash" night at the lighthouse. In the custom of many other Newfoundland women, Caroline Foran always made hash on Monday from Sunday dinner leftovers. Just as they sat down to supper, Mrs. Foran sensed that something was different that evening. Getting up from the supper table, she looked out the kitchen window, searching for some clue as to why she felt a strange unexplainable sensation that something was about to happen. Unable to sit down until her curiosity was satisfied, she went into her bedroom to take a look across the waters of Placentia Bay. There was nothing out of the ordinary to be seen, yet Caroline had an uneasy, eerie feeling that something was wrong. Before she turned to go back to the kitchen, the house began to tremble.

Back at the kitchen table, Francis Foran's older stepbrother, Ronald, had been keeping an eye on his mother's strange behaviour and needed no further convincing that something was going to happen. Ron, who had been a father-like figure to the younger Forans since their dad died, took charge. Ordering the children out of the house immediately, Ron ran to his bedroom. Before Francis left the kitchen, he observed his brother do something that he still laughs about. "Ron ran into his bedroom and grabbed a small sum of money he had put away there and the few dollars he had in his room, he gave to my mother. To this day, we've never had an explanation for that action. Perhaps he though the house was going to crumble with him in it."

Whether Ron thought the house was crumbling to the ground or not was the last thing on anyone's mind that evening. Scrambling from the dinner table, the family ran from the house as fast as they could. In the yard their initial fear changed to bewilderment. The Forans couldn't see anything to explain why the buildings were trembling like leaves on a tree in a Point Latine breeze. The strangest thing of all was that while buildings were shaking, the ground seemed perfectly still. In his writings, Brother Foran remembers that evening as an exciting but strange event:

> We moved out in front of the barn and watched as Ron went up the (light) tower. The top had been toppled from the kerosene light and the lamp was burning out of control. Ron threw the lamp out the small door in the tower. He then lit the spare lamp and came back to us.
>
> We somehow connected the shaking of the house with the fire in the light tower. Ron went to the hill to visit the Powers — to visit Pauline to be exact — and also to get the news. The stories he brought back left us even more confused. All the houses had felt the tremor. Most people attributed it to a chimney fire and threw salt down their chimneys (to put out the fire).

Confusion reigned for the rest of the night. As people compared stories, they realized that there were no chimney fires in Argentia that evening, yet they all felt the same tremors. Someone also noted that there was an unusually high tide about two hours after the houses shook.

Francis Foran doesn't remember anything about high tides, but he does remember his disappointment when they were finally allowed back into the house to finish supper. The family cat had all but cleaned off their dinner plates.

It was not until the next day the Forans heard the news that a powerful underwater earthquake had occurred 150 miles south of Newfoundland. The quake, measuring 7.2 on the Richter scale, caused a huge tidal wave that came ashore on the southern tip of the Burin Peninsula, about sixty miles southwest of the Point Latine lighthouse. The tidal wave caused massive destruction over a forty-mile stretch of communities from Rock Harbour to Lamaline.

The first tremors from the epicentre reached Burin at 5:00 p.m. and lasted five minutes, resulting in exceptionally low water levels on the southern tip of the peninsula. At 7:30 p.m. a tidal wave, or tsunami, of between thirty-five to fifty feet washed ashore. The waves, travelling at a speed of eighty miles per hour from the epicentre, reached the peninsula at a speed of sixty-five miles per hour, creating exceptionally high seas in the area until 10:00 p.m.

Twenty-seven deaths were attributed to the tidal wave and loss of property amounted to over $1,000,000. In addition, telegraph lines connecting the peninsula and St. John's were severed during the earthquake. Cable lines between Newfoundland and New York were damaged or inoperative. A total of twenty-eight breaks were reported in more than a dozen oceanic cables near the epicentre.

Although the ocean near Point Latine swelled much higher than normal high-tide levels, the only damage was a broken lighthouse lamp and a ruined Monday evening supper.

I Remember the Good

With the exception of a tidal wave and the image of battleships in front of the lighthouse, life for the Forans of Point Latine was much like life for most other lightkeepers, especially those who lived near a community. Sunday was always a busy day when women and young girls from Argentia would visit. They came to talk mostly, but often took pictures of the lighthouse. Evenings were a time for men callers. There were four Foran girls so there were plenty of what Brother Francis calls "attractions" for the young men of the area.

Anytime there was a visitor in town, the Forans could expect to see Father Adrian John Dee. Father Dee bundled his visitors in his old car and headed out over the bumpy road to the lightstation. "Mom always spotted the car as it drove along the Pond Head road. It gave her time to remove her apron and tidy up an already tidy house," Francis Foran recalls, smiling. Unfortunately, Mrs. Foran never kept a guest book. It would have been a wonderful "who's who" list of dignitaries who visited the Argentia area in those days.

Several American newcomers working on the Naval Base were quick to discover the welcome mat at the Latine lighthouse. One man, a Mr. Hunt, liked the place so much that he and his wife boarded with Mrs. Foran for several months. A cook from one of the mess halls visited from time to time, usually bringing home-baked pies. Brother Foran remembers one day when his mother was not in the mood to entertain visitors. When she saw the cook coming with another pie she locked the door. Obviously perturbed by the reception he had received, the cook threw the pie into Duck Pond before walking back to the Base.

Today, Brother Francis Foran smiles when he talks about his impressionable years growing up in the Point Latine lighthouse. It was a simple life and there were times his widowed mother required considerable imagination and ingenuity to stretch the food basket to feed her children. But they always made it through the tough times. For all the varied times he had on Point Latine, he remembers the good. And, as he would write in his later years, there are many special images that linger still:

> One of my favourites was a sailing dory, its jib and mainsail filled with the offshore breeze, scudding around Point Latine. Sitting on the front thwart (seat) was the younger

member of the crew of two and in the stern, the skipper, steering the dory with an oar. Both men were dressed in yellow oilskins. The older one smoked a fishermen's pipe, with the tobacco well packed and the screw top keeping the light from blowing away.

Chapter Eight

The Graveyard of the Atlantic

Cape Race

"My God, Gray, the *Titanic* has struck a berg!"

Supposedly, that's what wireless operator Jack Goodwin said to his colleague Walter Gray on the night of April 14, 1912.

Goodwin, Gray and Robert Hunston were on duty at the Cape Race wireless station when the *Titanic's* radio operator, Jack Phillips, keyed the most famous SOS in history. Many historical accounts of the first transmission from the sinking ship read: "CDQ – have struck iceberg — sinking fast — come to our assistance — Position; 41° 46' N 50° 14' W — MGY —."

According to a handwritten logbook record by Robert Hunston that night, there were several earlier transmissions from Jack Phillips about the sinking. According to Hunston, the *Titanic's* position was first given as 41° 44' N 50° 24' W, about 380 miles SSE of Cape Race. Hunston's logbook claims the transmission stating the vessel was in position 41° 46' N 50°14' W was a "corrected" position which placed the liner's location five or six miles away from the original set of coordinates.

Additional entries in the Cape Race logbook by Robert Hunston in the spring of 1912 tell of stern warnings from the British and Newfoundland governments to wireless operators on Cape Race. With forceful reminders that operators were sworn to secrecy, the government papers suggested dire consequences if an operator dared tell anyone about what they gleaned from their communications with the *Titanic* on the night of the sinking.

The governments were concerned about several issues immediately after the sinking. History states that Jack Goodwin first heard the distress signal from the famous White Star liner and immediately relayed the information to his colleagues. But that's not the way everyone remembers it. According to people working at Cape Race that night, Goodwin, Gray and Hunston were, in fact, on duty when the first message came in, but were taking a break, and were away from their posts.

It had been a busy evening for the three Cape Race operators, partly because of a deluge of messages from the *Titanic*. Passengers on the luxury liner, especially the rich and famous, were amused by the idea of sending messages from the ship to their friends in America. Many of the messages were frivolous ramblings that nevertheless had to be sent immediately, even though Jack Phillips was seriously overworked. Phillips and his assistant, twenty-one-year-old Harold Bride, had handled more than 250 passenger messages since leaving England three days before. As they got closer to Cape Race, the first landfall in North America, passengers were more than ever attracted to the lure of sending messages. Hardly able to keep up with the passenger traffic, Phillips, tired from celebrating his birthday the night before, grew irritated with fellow wireless operator Cyril Evans, onboard the ship *Californian.*

Just before the *Titanic* struck the iceberg, Evans was waiting anxiously to send an important message to the *Titanic.* After waiting for nearly an hour, Evans grew tired and interrupted the Titanic-to-Cape Race transmission to send his message. His transmission was interrupted. "Shut up, shut up, I'm busy with Cape Race," Phillips shot back. Miffed at what he considered an unwarranted heavy-handed response, Evans closed down his set for the night and went to bed.

If that exchange had not happened, the course of history might have been significantly altered. Cyril Evans had interrupted the *Titanic*-to-Cape Race transmission to inform the ship of dangerous icebergs in the area. Also, had Jack Phillips not been so tired and irritable and, subsequently, rude to Cyril Evans, it is possible the *Californian* operator might have been still at his work station when the distress call was sent out a short while later. When Jack Phillips was ordered by the *Titanic*'s Captain Smith to issue a mayday, the *Californian* was within sight of the *Titanic*, just fifteen miles away. As the *Californian* lay dead in the water waiting for daylight before attempting to proceed through the ice-infested North Atlantic, Cyril Evans' wireless set was silent.

Back at Cape Race, the three operators had successfully forwarded all the "Marconigrams" received from the *Titanic*. Thinking that everything had calmed down for the night, they decided to take a well-deserved break for a few minutes. They didn't leave the station unattended though. Controls were left in the hands of Jimmy Myrick, a teenager who was fascinated by wireless communications. At fourteen, Jimmy was not old enough to be hired as an operator, but there was no doubt that he was an "operator-in-training" for what everyone knew was his chosen vocation. Knowing Jimmy's competency was nearly equal to their own, the radio operators asked Jimmy if he'd like to take control while they stepped out for a few minutes. The young lad was thrilled to have an opportunity to sit in front of the operations panel by himself.

Jack Goodwin, Walter Grey and Robert Hunston had barely time to boil water for a mug of tea when Jimmy Myrick came rushing through the door saying that he had received a message that the *Titanic* had struck an iceberg and was sinking. Unable to believe their ears, the three men were back in their positions within minutes.

It's likely that the only historical significance to that story is that it was not Jack Goodwin who first heard the distress signal from the *Titanic*. Instead, it was a boy who was never recognized for his proper place in history. No one dared breathe a word about the incident because there were fears of serious repercussions if it became known that an untrained boy was at the controls instead of qualified wireless operators.

There was more at stake than the careers of three wireless operators. Politicians in England and Newfoundland feared that lawyers arguing over insurance claims might twist and contort the facts in endless and expensive court battles. Only now, nearly a hundred years later, are people talking openly about Jimmy Myrick and his connection to the greatest marine disaster in the history of the world.

Aunt Anna's Antenna

The Cape Race radio station is also known for other historical significance. It was none other than Guglielmo Marconi himself who set up the first wireless station there. After successfully completing the first transatlantic wireless transmission from Signal Hill in St. John's to Cornwall, England in December 1901, Marconi turned his attention to developing wireless stations in the United States, Canada and Newfoundland. In 1902 the famous inventor set up a small station at Cape Race. When the original building burned to the ground two years later, a new and bigger station was built on the same site. The Cape Race station would soon become one of the most important marine communication links in North America.

Dave Myrick tells a funny story about one of Marconi's many trips to Cape Race. The son of lighthouse keeper Jerry Myrick, Dave grew up on the cape. He remembers listening to his older relatives and friends telling a yarn about an elderly woman named Anna Perry who fell down and broke several bones. Mrs. Perry's nephew worked on the construction of Marconi's station. During a visit from Marconi, the young man was telling the inventor about his aunt's misfortune. "My Aunt Anna fell down and got all broke up."

Fixated on the world and language of telecommunications, the great inventor first appeared puzzled by the young man's remarks. Certain that no one on Cape Race had yet been involved in wireless communications, he laughed at the young man. "Antenna," Marconi sneered, "my good fellow, are you trying to tell me that you had an antenna here on Cape Race and that it has fallen and has been broken?"

The Graveyard

While several capes in North America have been called Graveyard of the Atlantic, Cape Race has probably witnessed more marine accidents than any other headland on the continent. Known to European fishermen and emigrants since the early 1800s as "the first

Courtesy Canadian Coast Guard, Fisheries and Oceans

Cape Race

landfall," Cape Race was either a blessing or a curse to mariners. It was known to the Portuguese as Cabo Raso meaning "flat cape," but most people gave it their own title, depending on the weather and the seas on the day their ship drew near the first landfall.

On a clear day in summer, Cape Race is a place of rugged beauty. In the thick of an infamous Grand Banks fog, the stark black cliffs are terrifying. Thousands of sailors have approached the foreboding fog-bound cliffs holding their breath. They hoped they were near enough for a glimpse of the headland to give them their bearings to adjust course for the next leg of their journey to Canada or New England. At the same time, they were praying they were far enough offshore to escape collision, and almost certain death, against some of the oldest and most jagged rocks on the North American Continent. All too often, the latter was their fate.

As was often the case, it took a string of tragedies to convince government of the need to build a lighthouse on Cape Race. In one of those accidents, forty-nine people, mostly Germans, perished in August 1840 when the *Florence,* struck the cliffs just west of the cape. The 200-ton American brigantine left the Netherlands on July 21, carrying sixteen German families from Rotterdam, bound for the New World. On the morning of August 9, after nearly three weeks at sea, Captain Edward Rose stood at the helm of the square-rigger, wondering how close he was to Cape Race. Fog was as thick as mud, but Captain Rose had made the trip many times before and carefully watched for telltale signs that land was drawing near. His finely tuned sense of smell told him he was nearing land. Scents of animals, woods and boglands wafted on the westerly winds. When land birds appeared above his ship, the captain sent a crewman to the bowsprit as a lookout. But it was no use. Totally blanketed in fog, the sailor didn't see a thing until the *Florence* smashed against a cliff near Cape Race.

Although winds were light, a steady swell kept pushing the thirty-year-old ship against the rocks. Captain Rose ordered women and children into the only two lifeboats the vessel had onboard. Thirty-eight passengers made it to safety, but without lifeboats to board forty-nine others, including Captain Rose and his crew, died as the *Florence* broke in pieces under the crush of the swell.

With the loss of nearly forty emigrants in addition to the crew of the *Florence,* pressure mounted on government to construct a light-house at Cape Race. Although the British Admiralty sent a man to view the area in 1847, there was indecision about whether Cape Race was the best place to establish a light. For some reason the government seemed to favour nearby Cape Pine as a more suitable location.

While the British politicians argued over an appropriate site for a lighthouse, the waters off Cape Race became increasingly crowded and dangerous as the emigrant trade from Europe to New York increased dramatically. More ships were lost near Cape Race — two of them in the fall of 1854.

In September that year, another large emigrant ship, *City of Philadelphia,* ran ashore just a few hundred feet north of Cape Race. Luckily, the seas were calm and all 540 people onboard made it to the safety of the beach in Chance Cove.

About three weeks later, two ocean-going ships collided just off Cape Race. The fate of many of their crew and passengers was not so fortunate. An American ship, *Arctic,* with 381 passengers onboard, was struck by a French vessel, *Vesta.* The four-year-old luxury liner *Arctic* was the pride of the Collins Line (New York and Liverpool United States Steamship Company). In February 1852, the new steamship had made history with a record crossing from New York to Liverpool in nine days, seventeen hours and twelve minutes. But the superior speed of the large liner was not enough to outrun the danger of a Cape Race fog. On September 27, 1854, the wooden-hulled *Arctic* was badly holed by the iron-hulled *Vesta* in the collision. The *Arctic* quickly sank to the bottom of the ocean, taking more than 300 people with her.

With the list of casualties near Cape Race mounting every month, the British Secretary of State, Sir George Grey, wrote Newfoundland's Governor LeMarchant the following spring:

> ...the importance of building a lighthouse at Cape Race; having attracted the attention of Her Majesty's Government, I have to inform you that Parliament will be asked this session to apply a sum of £5000 for that purpose.

Eighteen months later, on December 15, 1856, the first light from Cape Race was lit. Retired sea captain William Hally was hired as the first principal lightkeeper.

To the amazement of many, it was soon discovered that even a lighthouse could not prevent disaster from occurring at Cape Race. Just ten days after the light went into operation, the cargo ship *Welsford,* bound for Liverpool from New Brunswick, became lost in darkness and thick fog. Around suppertime on Christmas Day the ship struck the rocks just below the brand new lighthouse. Hally and an assistant lightkeeper got a line down the 125-foot cliff to the ship and managed to hoist four of *Welsford's* crew to safety. Sadly, the twenty-two remaining crewmembers died attempting to get to shore.

Because of new technology in the late 1800s, the waters around

Cape Race became even more congested shortly after the installation of the light. When the New York Associated Press learned about a new telegraph link that had been established between St. John's and New York, they devised a clever scheme to beat their competition with news from Europe. The NYAP set up a system whereby mail boats from southern Newfoundland would rendezvous with trans-atlantic steamers just off Cape Race. Barrels containing news from Europe were lowered over the side into the waiting mail boats. The mail boats took the newspapers to St. John's where the news was telegraphed to New York. That way, the NYAP had the news ten days earlier than their competitors who had to wait for the steamers to arrive in New York.

If it was foggy or if seas were too rough to make a transfer, the watertight canisters were simply thrown overboard and fishermen were paid the handsome sum of £5 sterling for every barrel retrieved and taken to Cape Race. Fishermen soon realized that collecting news barrels was more lucrative than fishing. As a result, very few barrels ever went missing, even after several consecutive days of heavy fog or raging storms. Their keenly honed sense of reading tide and wind directions always told fishermen exactly where to look for a floating barrel of paper.

More Than a Light

As marine traffic off Cape Race increased, so did the need for a fog alarm to accompany the lighthouse. But, like the lighthouse, the fog alarm would not be built until the world was shocked by yet another major tragedy.

The three-masted iron steamship, *Anglo Saxon,* was built in Scot-land for the Allen Shipping Line in 1860. A large vessel, she boasted speeds exceeding ten knots, ideal for the emigrant trade to the New World from England, Scotland and Ireland. On April 16, 1863 she left Liverpool with eighty-six crewmembers and 360 passengers bound first for Ireland and then Quebec City.

It was an uneventful crossing. Like Captain Rose on the ill-fated *Florence* twenty-three years earlier, Captain Burgess intuitively knew when he was approaching Cape Race, although he couldn't see the first landfall. After breakfast on Monday morning, April 27, the captain of the *Anglo Saxon* peered into the dense fog and ordered the engine room to reduce speed just in case land was near. Land was nearer than the good captain thought. Just after eleven o'clock that morning, it loomed large directly in front of the ship. Captain Burgess immediately ordered "full-astern" but it was too late. The big ship grounded on a reef, just yards from the entrance to Clam Cove three miles north of Cape Race.

At first Captain Burgess thought he might be able to free his ship. While the bow was fairly tightly wedged on the reef, the stern was floating. Attempts to reverse the ship sealed her fate once and for all. With engines full astern, the liner's stern swung to the starboard and went hard aground on several large rocks. As seas pounded against the side of the stricken vessel, Captain Burgess realized that although the beach was only a few hundred yards from his ship, disaster was imminent. Even as he ordered the crew to prepare to launch the lifeboats, Burgess knew that getting ashore in the rough seas would be very difficult. But worse than that, he also knew there were only enough lifeboats for about half the passengers. As the ship began to founder, several lifeboats managed to get away but one was smashed to pieces when it became tangled in the vessel's crumpled riggings. As waves tossed them unmercifully against the iron hull of the *Anglo Saxon*, everyone in the lifeboat died.

Lightkeeper William Hally and his assistant George Hewitt were alerted to the plight of the ill-fated liner by the constant blasts of the ship's whistle when she ran aground. They arrived on the hill overlooking Clam Cove just in time to see several crewmembers trying to swim ashore. Several of the crew had tied ropes around their waists with the other end still attached to the ship. Three of the men made it to land and, using the ropes they'd brought with them, managed to rig a bosun's chair to the ship. Women and children were the first to be hoisted over the bow.

As Hally and Hewitt scrambled down the steep cliffs of Clam Cove, they knew they could be dealing with people who were dead or dying. Their first instincts were to help save the approximately eighty people who had made it to shore on the bosun's chair and were now stranded on the icy beach below. Soaked and shivering in freezing temperatures, the survivors barely had enough strength to climb the rocky cliff to the comfort of the lighthouse buildings. Working as quickly as they could to rescue those who made it to shore, the two lightkeepers could only watch helplessly as the *Anglo Saxon* began to founder and slip from the rocks into deeper water. Two hundred and thirty-seven people died either trying to reach the rocky shores of Clam Cove or, like Captain Burgess, going down with the ship.

The next day William Hally and George Hewitt began the gruesome task of recovering dozens of bodies that were washing up on the beach. The lightkeepers buried the bodies on the hill overlooking Clam Cove with beach rocks marking their graves at both the head and feet. More than a hundred bodies could not be identified.

The inquiry into the *Anglo Saxon* disaster not only called for a fog alarm system for Cape Race, but also noted that the lighthouse needed upgrading. After several years of bickering among politicians, a powerful fog whistle was finally placed on the cape in 1872.

While there is no doubt the lighthouse and fog alarm system alerted hundreds of ships away from certain disaster, Cape Race would continue to live up its reputation as Graveyard of the Atlantic. A story in the St John's *Evening Telegram* on March 4, 1904 claimed that more than 2000 people had died in ninety-four shipwrecks near Cape Race between 1864 to 1904. In 1901 there was an epidemic of shipwrecks near the cape; ships of all sizes were practically piling up on top of each other. That summer, no fewer than seven ships crashed to watery graves near the cape. One of them was the *Lusitania,* a large French cargo vessel carrying 440 passengers and crew. Unlike the more famous luxury liner *Lusitania* that was torpedoed by a German U-boat and sank on May 7, 1915, with the loss of nearly 1200 lives, there was no loss of life in the wreck of the cargo vessel *Lusitania* in 1901.

A Fine Place to Live

The early 1900s brought new additions to Cape Race. In 1904 a new marine wireless radio station was built on the hill near the lighthouse.

Operators at the "Marconi" station could communicate by Morse code with vessels hundreds of miles away. Three years later, the foghorn was replaced because the old alarm was often mistaken for a ship's whistle. A brand new diaphone alarm, powered by one of the largest steam compressors in the world, was installed in 1907.

Later the same year, the government built a brand new lighthouse on Cape Race. It was a commanding ninety-six foot iron tower that housed an immense lens capped by a huge copper dome. More than twice the height of the old structure, the new lighthouse, with eighty-five concrete steps spiralling up and around the sides of the tower, was one of the most sophisticated in the world. Consisting of four eight-foot lenses, the new light illuminated 1.5 million candlepower. The various pieces of equipment supporting the light weighed seven tons, including 1000 pounds of mercury.

With the construction of the new light, in addition to the elaborate fog whistle and two radio stations, Cape Race had grown to be a small town in the early to mid-1900s. There were as many as a dozen families living on the cape some years. They even had a small post office and a little two-room school that taught grades kindergarten to eleven. At one time there were more than thirty students attending the Cape Race School.

"Cape Race was a fine place to live," says Frank Myrick. Born on the cape in 1919, Frank worked there as a radio operator when he was a young man. He later moved to St. John's and became a Coast Guard technician installing light systems all around Newfoundland and Labrador. Like most people who grew up on lightstations, Frank Myrick has pleasant memories and enjoys talking about his adventures.

Although Frank was hailed a hero by most who knew him when he was a young man, he talks matter-of-factly about a time he risked his life attempting to save two fishermen. On Tuesday, March 24, 1936, Frank was helping his father at a job in the fog alarm building. As was customary for lightkeepers, Tom Myrick kept glancing toward the ocean as he went about his chores that foggy morning. Suddenly, Tom thought he saw something moving through the fog. Stopping his work, he strained to get another look but heavy fog obscured his view. Finally, the light breeze parted the fog long enough for Tom to see two men in a dory just off the cape. Moving outside to get a better look, Tom noticed the men had draped a coat over an oar they had placed upright in the dory. Recognizing the signal of men in trouble, the lightkeeper called his seventeen-year-old son, Frank, to take a look.

While his father ran to signal to the men that they had been sighted, Frank took note of weather and sea conditions. Winds were moderate but seas, in the aftermath of recent bad weather, were breaking dangerously over the rocks at the foot of the cape. When Tom returned he agreed with his son that it was too risky to attempt landing a dory on the cape. Attracting the dorymen's attention by waving a flag, Tom signalled them to follow him along the cliff to Big Cove, the safest place to come ashore in those conditions.

In the dory, Jimmy Frampton and his dory-mate, John Senior, were overwhelmed with joy to see the lightkeepers on top of the cliff. The two men from Tacks Beach in Placentia Bay had become separated from their schooner about eighty miles offshore while fishing on the Grand Banks in thick fog. At first they rowed their dory in no particular direction, hoping to come upon one of the fishing schooners in the area. After a day had passed and there was still no sound of schooners approaching them, they decided to try and reach land.

Without navigational aids, the men were only guessing at which direction was the right one. Day after day and night after night they rowed, but there was no sign of land or ships. Finally, five days after they last saw their schooner, the men heard the sound of water breaking over rocks. Cold beyond shivering and weak from hunger, they desperately tried to reach land in Cripple Cove near Trepassey, but the pounding surf was too powerful to safely row the small boat among the rocks to the shoreline. One large wave crashed over the dory, catching John Senior off guard, washing him overboard. Somehow Jimmy managed to steady the boat long enough to get his friend safely back in the dory and they headed out to the calmer waters of the open sea.

Staying as close to the sound of seas breaking on the shoreline as they dared, the two men rowed their dory another long day and night until finally they heard the drone of the Cape Race foghorn. Hoping that someone from the lighthouse would see them, the fishermen stayed close to the cape, never straying far from the sound of the fog alarm. When they saw Tom Myrick waving a flag on Tuesday morning, they thanked God and prayed that an end to their six-day ordeal would be near.

With renewed energy born of hope, the two Tacks Beach fishermen rowed their dory briskly in the direction signalled by the men walking along the cliffs above them. Finally they rounded a headland and approached the beach in Big Cove where Frank and Tom Myrick were waiting. Where the heavy swell rolled in over the shallow waters of Big Cove, the ocean turned into swirling surf, similar to the seas the two men had encountered in Cripple Cove on Saturday. This time, though, they were more willing to take the chance of riding the white water because help was just a few hundred feet away. To keep a close watch on what was happening in front of the boat, Jimmy Frampton decided to "sheave" the dory to land. Sheaving is the local term for the practice of rowing a dory by pushing instead of pulling the oars as the rower sits facing the bow in order to see what is ahead.

Things went well for a little while. Although the dory was tossed about like a cork, John managed to hang on with the little strength he had left, while Jimmy steadied the small boat with the oars. Primarily concerned with avoiding capsizing in seas that might wash across the sides of the dory, Jimmy didn't see the big wave rushing toward the boat directly behind them. By the time they heard the roar of an oncoming rogue-wave, it was too late to prepare for it. Within seconds the dory was tossed in the air end over end, landing upside down in the water.

On the beach, Tom and Frank Myrick watched in horror. They saw Jimmy rise to the surface but there was no sign of John. Aware there was not enough time to launch their own dory to try and rescue the men, Tom Myrick knew there was only one option. "Get out there and get those men in," he commanded his seventeen-year-old son.

Oblivious to the freezing temperatures and unconcerned about the dangers of trying to swim in the rock-infested, swirling waters,

Frank quickly tied a small rope around his waist, handing the free end to his father, and dived in. After a few minutes swimming, Frank was able to grab Jimmy Frampton who was clinging to the overturned dory. It was a struggle, but the young man managed to tow the fisherman through the foam to the beach. Undaunted by the surf, Frank turned around and headed back through the white water again. As he approached the dory, Frank saw John Senior floating face-down in the water. He managed to get one arm around the unconscious man and, with the other arm, started swimming back to shore.

Despite Frank's courageous rescue effort, it was too late for John Senior. As they lay him on the beach, it was obvious he was already dead. A deep bloodied gash on his head indicated that something, perhaps an oar or a rock had struck him when the dory flipped over.

Not surprisingly, Jimmy Frampton developed pneumonia after spending six miserably cold damp days in a small dory without food or water, but after several days resting in the Myrick household he was well enough to travel home to Tacks Beach.

There is an ironic but sad epilogue to the story of Jimmy Frampton. After surviving incredible odds that week in March, 1936, he died at sea just two years later when the boom on a schooner mast broke loose and knocked him overboard.

Frank Myrick recounts other dramatic adventures with nonchalance; high drama seemed to follow the man from Cape Race. He remembers a night sometime in the 1940s when he was doing the midnight shift at the station. Around five or six o'clock in the morning, the door opened and a half dozen men walked in. The six were survivors from a schooner that had sunk the day before. They had rowed ashore in a dory. He also talks about the morning of May 31, 1977 when the *William Carson* sank off Cartwright, Labrador. Frank was working onboard the Canadian Coast Guard ship *Sir Humphrey Gilbert* located about seventeen miles from St. Anthony when it received the call from Coast Guard Radio saying that the *Carson* was holed by ice and sinking. The marine radio operator in St. Anthony who received the distress call from the sinking ship was also the son of a lightkeeper. Clyde Roberts grew up on Belle Isle where his father, Fred Roberts, was lightkeeper for many years.

Fortunately, the rescue mission was not particularly traumatic for either Clyde Roberts or Frank Myrick. Unlike many ships that foundered in the area years ago, the *Carson* carried plenty of lifeboats. With a load capacity of more than 500 passengers, there were more than enough lifeboats for the forty-three crewmembers and thirty-seven passengers onboard at the time. While Clyde Roberts maintained permanent contact with the captain of the sinking vessel, the eighty men and women onboard were climbing safely into lifeboats. At the same time the *Gilbert* was speeding toward the ill-fated vessel to pick them up.

Frank remembers observing some of the thickest and hardest ice he'd ever seen that day. "Some of it was ten feet thick and so hard it was blue," he says. The evacuation of the ship went well and all hands were waiting in relative comfort when the rescue vessel *Gilbert* arrived on the scene.

The War Years

Frank Myrick's cousin, Cyril Myrick, also has memories of high drama. "I thoroughly enjoyed my young days growing up on the cape," says Cyril who worked as a marine radio operator on the cape for many years. Son of lighthouse keeper Pat Myrick, Cyril, born in the mid-1930s, especially remembers his school days and the excitement of the war years. "I even remember what the weather was like on Cape Race the day Hitler declared war," Cyril laughs. "I was only a boy of about five and a half years of age but I remember it was a calm overcast day on the cape." An avid radio listener in his youth, Cyril monitored every newscast during the war, plotting the movements of both the German and Allied forces on his world map.

Plotting the course of events in Europe was one thing, but the young Cyril Myrick saw the war come much closer to home. "We'd be in school and someone would say there's a convoy coming into view. When I'd look out the window, there were times the sea would be black with warships going by the cape."

The Cape Race lighthouse became as beneficial to the Germans as it was to the Allies during World War II. The light was a directional beacon for military as well as civilian ships, so German submarine commanders took advantage of the frequent concentrations of Allied vessels in the area. In fact, the presence of German U-Boats was so common there were rumours that some Cape Race lightkeepers were paid by the Germans to supply information about the whereabouts of Allied ships. The rumours were never considered as anything more than idle gossip.

The fact that the Germans benefitted from the lighthouse beacon gave comfort to the residents of Cape Race. Frances Myrick, Cyril's sister, says the older people assured the children that they had nothing to fear because the Germans needed the light and wouldn't do anything to harm the people who kept the light operating. The children understood their parents' logic and, although they took comfort from it, they were sometimes a little nervous about having the enemy so near. "It was nothing to see a submarine periscope slicing through the water just off the cape every day," Frances says. One day Frances and some friends picked up a German book in one of the coves near the cape, a chilling reminder that Germans were never far away. For some people on the cape, it felt as if the Germans were secretly watching them all the time.

Frances laughs about the evening she thought the Germans attacked her home. It was a bitterly cold winter night and, for fun, she and her brothers were putting on a "concert" in their living room. Cyril was up on the stage, otherwise known as the couch, singing songs and reciting poetry. Although Cyril was standing directly in front of the window, no one could see outside because the blind was drawn.

However, from the outside, the yellow blind didn't hinder his brother Ern from figuring out what going on. Arriving home from visiting friends, Ern easily recognized the silhouette of his younger brother standing on the stage. Thinking he would give his siblings a little scare, Ern knocked on the window right behind Cyril. Forgetting the bitterly cold temperature, Ern tapped the window too hard and the frozen windowpane practically exploded as it shattered into a thousand pieces. "We got the fright of our lives — we were sure the

Germans had landed and were attacking us!" Frances says, laughing at her wonderful memories.

Cyril remembers one childhood day above all others. He was in school when someone noticed a huge convoy of warships stretching from half a mile off Cape Race to as far as one could see on the horizon. The sight was so impressive that the teacher decided to take the children outdoors to view the spectacle. It was a day Cyril Myrick will never forget. "Just as the convoy was abeam the cape, all hell broke loose," he says. "Guns were firing and depth charges were going off — it was an earth-shattering noise — so loud and powerful it seemed like the cliffs themselves were rattling." An hour or so later, when it appeared the excitement was over, the teacher herded the children back to school. Just as everyone was seated, a thunderous explosion rocked the little two-room schoolhouse, rattling the windows.

Rushing outside to see what had caused the explosion, Cyril saw a large mushroom of black smoke rising from the ocean just off Long Point, south of Cape Race. "All the commotion was over two or three German submarines that suddenly appeared in the midst of the convoy," Cyril says. Somehow, the subs managed to elude the depth charges and gunshots and ran for cover inside Long Point. Thinking the Germans were well out to sea by then, the convoy was not expecting the torpedo that was speeding directly toward one of the corvettes. "He struck her directly amidships and the corvette was blown to hell; smoke was rising at least 300 feet into the air," Cyril recalls.

Cyril Myrick remembers another ship that was torpedoed off Cape Race during WWII — one that took the life of a friend. Pete Bishop worked at the marine radio station on the cape, but the young man from the fishing community of Wesleyville in Bonavista Bay preferred life on the sea. When he heard there was a job opening onboard a Canadian Merchant Marine ship, he jumped at the chance and took a job working in the engine room. As fate would have it, Pete's ship was torpedoed just off Cape Race, the place where he had worked for several years. "Down there in the engine room; he never had a chance; the ship went down within minutes," Cyril recalls sadly.

It was common for lightkeepers and their families to care for survivors of ships that were wrecked in storms, and on Cape Race it was not unusual to have company come after a ship had been torpedoed by German submarines. Cyril and his sister Frances remember two Norwegian seamen who came to stay with them after a submarine sank their cargo ship. All but two people survived. Cyril remembers when the police officer from Trepassey came to get the survivors from the Norwegian ship. The officer intended to put the men in the back of an old truck without as much as a railing to hold on to. From the cape, the officer was to drive the survivors to Trepassey where a ship was waiting to take them home. Mrs. Myrick was not impressed with the battered old truck and didn't like the idea of treating people like cattle. She informed the officer of her opinion. "Those men have been through enough already; they don't need to be treated that way," she scolded him. Happy to be going home, the survivors accepted the ride anyway, regardless of the condition of their taxi.

Frances remembers another side to the story of their Norwegian visitors. She remembers one of them, a tall good-looking officer, sitting in their dining room, singing and playing guitar. But most of all she remembers his magnificent navy-blue coat. "It was full of shiny brass buttons," she says. When the officer was leaving, he gave the coat to her father Pat in appreciation for the family's hospitality.

Stories from the war years on Cape Race seem endless. Cyril remembers another time when a Canadian military airplane crash-landed in the ocean near Chance Cove, a few minutes boat ride north of the cape. It was late at night and everyone in the Myrick home was asleep. Cyril's mother was the first to awake to an unusual noise. Once alert, she recognized the sound of an unusually low-flying airplane. Thinking it was nothing more than an aircraft flying over the cape, Mrs. Myrick joked to her husband that "If that plane comes any closer to this house, I'll have a pilot in bed with me tonight." Moments later the plane crashed into the ocean just off Chance Cove.

As it turned out, the pilot didn't need to come ashore for lodging that night. With a little bit of luck and a large amount of skill, he landed the aircraft smoothly in the water. To the astonishment of Sol Reid, captain of a fishing boat moored in Chance Cove for the night, the pilot somehow managed to manoeuvre the aircraft in the water until the tip of the wing came within inches of the vessel. Incredibly, the flight crew simply walked out on the wing of the plane and jumped onboard the fishing vessel. "To think that the plane was not even a seaplane, it was amazing — they didn't even get their feet wet," Cyril says, still shaking his head in disbelief.

At first Captain Reid thought he must have been looking at a Catalina Flying Boat. However, taking a closer look at the floating aircraft, he was amazed to discover that the plane was a Canadian Air Force Douglas bomber. It was a fascinating sight for young Cyril Myrick too. He remembers watching in awe as a Canadian Navy corvette and a cargo ship arrived on the scene the next day and attempted to tow the airplane out to sea. They were obviously trying to salvage the perfectly intact aircraft. Cyril still wonders why they didn't simply hoist the plane onboard the cargo ship from the location where it had landed. Instead, they towed the plane further offshore into rougher seas. A wave caught the wing tip, flipped the aircraft over, and water quickly filled the cabin. A few minutes later, the big bomber slipped beneath the surface.

Christmas on the cape holds a special place in Cyril's memory. "The adults were always extremely family-oriented and during the Christmas holidays they would go all-out to make it very special," he says. Dividing the age groups into "believers" and "non-believers," Cyril loves to talk about the days when all the kids his age were definitely believers.

His father started the proceedings every Christmas Eve around suppertime. Always making sure to check on the fog whistle just after Christmas Eve supper, Mr. Myrick would come back to the house around 6:30 p.m. in a foul mood, grumbling about an old white-bearded so-and-so who had caused a lot of work for him in the fog-alarm building that afternoon. "He was down there again makin' his usual mess," he'd fuss. When Cyril and the other children asked who he was talking about, Mr. Myrick would launch into a convincing story about how every Christmas Eve this certain old man would show up at the fog alarm building. The bearded fat man in a red suit and black boots was always full of snow and seemed to really enjoy sneaking into the fog alarm building, which was warmed by the huge pot-bellied stove that heated the steam to operate the fog horn. "What a bloody mess he made down there again this evening; there's big puddles of water where snow from his clothes was melting all over the place," Pat Myrick would say, pretending to be extremely upset with the unwelcome visitor. Young Cyril Myrick and the other children knew from the description that the visitor was Santa Claus and they'd get very angry with their father for being unkind to the old gentleman. "I was afraid that if Santa knew that Dad was upset, he might not come to our house later that night," Cyril recalls.

If Cyril was tormented by his father's "snowy Santa" routine, Pat Myrick and all the other fathers on Cape Race more than made up for their bit of light-hearted fun later on Christmas Eve night. That's when their creativity really blossomed. The men would go as far as saving hooves from cows slaughtered earlier for their winter's supply of meat. On Christmas Eve, after the children were asleep, the men would climb up on the roofs of the houses with barrel staves and cloven hooves in tow. With the hooves tied to a stick, they would strategically drop them in the snow, leaving a perfect imitation of reindeer tracks walking across the rooftop. The staves were used to create the ski-type impression of sleigh runners in the snow. On Christmas morning the children would be taken up to the rooftop to view the tracks of the sleigh and cloven hooves that always, magically, ended alongside the chimney. "With convincing antics like that, we were pretty old before we began to have doubts," Cyril confesses with a grin.

New Technology — Safer Shipping

As electronic technology vastly improved from the 1950s to the 1970s, the number of shipping accidents rapidly declined. New radar and communications electronics kept ships' officers fully informed of their positions at all times. Where once ships literally sank on top of each other, barely a shipping incident occurs anymore. An exception to that generalization happened in 1982 when lightkeeper Fred Osbourne assisted in the prevention of a possible disaster involving the fishing trawler *Fame V*. There was no loss of life and the light-keeper was never at risk, probably because of advanced communications technology.

As she headed toward the Grand Banks, the trawler, owned by the Lake Group of Companies in St. John's, broke down on Tuesday evening, March 2, about a mile from the cape. As soon as he was notified about the incident, Fred went outside to check things out. It was shortly after 9:00 p.m., long after sunset, but a bright half-moon illuminated the sky. Fred saw the dragger drifting a short distance southwest of the cape. The dragger was not in any immediate danger; winds were light and seas were not threatening to push the vessel ashore. Going back to the lightstation, Fred opened a nearly constant communications link with the vessel's owners and Coast Guard Radio. He watched as the container ship *Cabot* swung by and took a look. Although the large vessel nearly circled the *Fame V*, Fred was surprised when the *Cabot* left the scene without any apparent attempt to assist the stricken dragger.

At about 10:00 p.m., seas became higher as winds increased from the south to twenty-five or thirty knots. The change in weather was bad news for the *Fame V*. Without power, the dragger started drifting quickly toward dangerous rocks near the cape. As Fred kept every-one informed about where the dragger was heading, the engineers somehow managed to regain power for a few minutes, long enough to move the ship about a half mile from the rocks and out of harm's way for a little while longer. "It was getting a little tense for a while though; she was only a few feet away from some pretty ugly rocks when he got her going," Fred says. Fred didn't know it that night but the *Fame V* actually struck bottom. Fortunately the captain managed to get away from the rocks before going hard aground.

Tensions mounted when Fred saw a life raft drifting near the cape. Certain the raft belonged to the *Fame V*, Fred grabbed a rope and flashlight and followed the shoreline to where it appeared the raft might drift ashore. Shouting, Fred asked if there was anyone in the raft. There was no response. The raft didn't come ashore and as it drifted by the headland, Fred watched helplessly, wondering if there were injured people inside the canopy. Terrified at the thought of the raft smashing against the cliffs, Fred ran back to the lightstation to make a phone call. He was immensely relieved to learn that the life raft was empty. It seems the crew was preparing the raft for quick boarding, just in case they were forced to abandon ship when it slipped over the side and drifted away.

Around midnight, Fred got word that an order had been sent to the crew of the *Fame V* to abandon ship. Fred watched as a twenty-five-man life raft was lowered over the side. But, before anyone could get in the raft, he saw the mast lights of another vessel, heading directly toward the *Fame V* full speed ahead. "It was amazing," Fred says. "He brought her in there whatever she could go and, just as he got in the right spot, he swung her hard around, directly into the wind, and cut his engines. It was just like he had brakes. When he stuck her up in the wind, she stopped flat, no more than 25 or 30 feet away right in the perfect position to get a line onboard." Shortly afterwards, the *Fame V* was being towed to port in St. John's.

Although Fred Osbourne's role in the rescue of the *Fame V* was relatively minor, the manager of the Lake Company was thankful the lightkeeper was on watch and describing each step of the proceedings from up on the cape. In a letter to Fred, company president Tim Eburne, wrote:

> Your efforts and contributions, I am sure, were vital to the rescue actions and instrumental in helping prevent a major disaster.

Although there was no loss of life in that incident, it was nonetheless a traumatic experience for Fred Osbourne. When he finally managed to get to bed around 3:00 a.m., images of twelve men in a raft being smashed against eighty-foot cliffs kept him awake all night.

New Adventures

The most noticeable decline in shipping accidents near Cape Race came in the 1960s. Eva Myrick says everything changed in those years. Wife of longtime lightkeeper Jim Myrick, Eva says captains became so confident in their navigational technology, they would often swing their ships close to the cape, even on foggy days, and give a couple of blasts on the ship's whistle as a greeting.

Eva's son Noel Myrick continues to carry on the family tradition of lightkeeping. Currently stationed at Cape Race where he grew up, Noel works in a very different environment than did his father, cousins and uncles. The only people on the cape are the two light-keepers on duty working their twenty-eight-day shifts. No one lives there anymore.

If you sit and listen to Noel Myrick and the other keepers talk about life on Cape Race today there won't be many stories about shipwrecks, but it won't be long before the conversation turns to modern day rescues and tragedies averted. They'll tell you about the day in July, 1990 when a boatload of teenagers was heading for Cripple Cove from Clam Cove and their engine broke down. Had Noel not been keeping a close watch on them, an uneventful story might have had a very different ending. As lightkeepers seem to do intuitively, Noel trained his binoculars on the group of about ten young men and women in a twenty-two-foot open boat as they steamed along the coastline. Everything appeared fine as Noel watched the boat disappear around a headland and toward Cripple Cove.

Noel Myrick was not obliged to concern himself with that boat anymore but as lightkeepers have been doing for years, he went the extra mile, in this case literally. While he had no reason to suspect anything would go wrong, he decided to get in his pickup truck and travel to Cripple Cove, just to be absolutely sure that everything was fine. Arriving there, Noel was surprised to discover the young people had not yet made it to the wharf. It wasn't stormy but the twenty-knot wind was from the south, meaning it was blowing toward the land. That worried Noel enough to ask a fisherman from the Cove if he would go out around the headland and check on the young people. The fisherman discovered the overdue boat without power and drifting quickly toward the rocky shoreline. Attaching a line to the boat the fisherman towed them to port without incident.

Fortunately, there is not much of a story from that incident — at least not much of a news story, but no one will ever know what the consequences for those young people might have been had it not been for the lightkeeper's vigilance.

There was no need to wonder about whether a life was saved on February 15, 1986 on Cape Race. There is no doubt that a young man from Trepassey would have died had it not been for the efforts of lightkeeper Tom Ryan.

It was -13 degrees Celsius at 7:00 a.m. when Tom heard a knock at the door of the lighthouse residence. A distraught young man named Pat Ward said his friend had slipped into the ocean while they were hunting saltwater birds at dawn. As Tom, a first-aid instructor, grabbed some warm clothes, the young man explained that his partner, Michael Kennedy, was in the frigid waters for at least half an hour before he managed to get him to the beach. After struggling to get his friend to the road at the top of the hill, Pat put Michael in the car where it was slightly warmer. Unfortunately, Pat, only fourteen at the time, couldn't drive the standard-shift vehicle and had to walk to get help.

When they arrived at the car, Tom knew within seconds that Michael was in an advanced state of hypothermia. "He was in a daze and gone beyond the stage of shivering and he was also totally incoherent," Tom says.

As soon as they were back inside the lighthouse residence, Tom and Pat removed Michael's wet clothes and wrapped him in blankets. Tom filled the bathtub and immersed him in lukewarm water, still wrapped in the blankets. After a few minutes had a passed, Tom thought it was time to take the man out of the tub, although there was still no indication that his condition was improving. A few minutes later Tom repeated the procedure. Finally, after approximately thirty minutes, Michael showed signs of recovery. "When he stopped babbling and started talking normally, I knew he was going to be all right," Tom smiles. Two hours later Michael Kennedy was strong enough to drive home to Trepassey.

Because lighthouses are linked to the ocean, the vast bulk of tragedy and rescue stories have been associated with vessels and sea people. But there have many incidents when lightkeepers have been called on to help someone in trouble on land. Noel Myrick was on duty one day at the Cape Race lighthouse when a man knocked on the door saying that his hunting partner had suffered what appeared to be a heart attack, about a mile from the lighthouse. Noel immediately contacted the RCMP and Coast Guard. A short while later a Search and Rescue helicopter was on the scene and airlifted the man to hospital where he made a full recovery. If there had been no lighthouse keeper in the area to take immediate action, the situation might not have turned out so happily.

If a community group from the Trepassey area gets it's way, tourists and the Newfoundland public will soon have an opportunity to see firsthand what life was like on Cape Race. Hoping the tremendous historical significance of the cape will attract thousands of people to travel there every year, the group has proposed a major restoration project. Their wish is to, once again, make Cape Race a towering beacon of hope by shining its brilliant history across the land to create much-needed work for a different brand of lighthouse people.

Chapter Nine

Tide's Point

Perhaps with the exception of a few romantics, living on top of a rock that is constantly subjected to the Atlantic Ocean environment is not what most people want for their children. However, almost without exception, the sons and daughters of lighthouse keepers talk glowingly about their early years. Like Francis Foran of Point Latine and Cyril Myrick of Cape Race, lighthouse children were a contented lot. Irene (Dicks) Pearcey summed up the thoughts of most of them in an essay she wrote about her childhood on Tide's Point on the Burin Peninsula. "We felt free and secure," she said.

Without the distractions of the hustle and bustle of large towns and cities, life in a community of two or three families was absolute freedom. The community was theirs alone. Their feelings of security came from exceptionally strong family bonds. "Family was every-thing — we all relied on one another — that's all we had," they point out.

Like many children who grew up on lightstations, Irene and her eight brothers and sisters had deep roots in the lightkeeping lifestyle. Her grandfather, Michael Dicks, was the first lighthouse keeper on Tide's Point when the light was constructed there in 1912. Irene's father, John Dicks, took over from his Dad in 1925. John stayed there until 1949 when he took a new job with the Coast Guard in St. John's.

John Kavanagh echoes Irene's sentiments about the good life on Tide's Point. Hired by Irene's father in 1946, Kavanagh spent nearly forty years working at the little Placentia Bay lighthouse — "not bad for a job that was decided on the toss of a coin," he says. Kavanagh and another man were competing for the job but John Dicks couldn't decide who should be the successful applicant. Both men had all the required credentials. Finally, Dicks came up with the only fair system he knew. In an interview in 1994, John Kavanagh told newspaper reporter Lisa Young that John Dicks gave the other applicant a fifty-cent piece and told him to "go find John Kavanagh and toss for it." Dicks also suggested that the loser should get the fifty-cent piece. John Kavanagh won the toss that day. He called heads and when the coin landed on the ground, heads it was. The other man graciously accepted the luck of the draw, took his fifty cents and bought a plug of tobacco.

Nearly fifty years later, John Kavanagh described his years on Tide's Point as a good life — a life he was sad to leave when it came time to retire. Reminiscing about the old days, John Kavanagh talks about the worries of raising children on top of a cliff. Kavanagh and other lightkeepers remember their lightkeeping days as a time when parents kept constant vigils on their children, knowing that one misplaced step could be fatal. They talk about lonely times and managing to find things to do to keep everyone occupied. Like their children, lightkeepers constantly hark back to the overwhelming sense of family that tied everyone together in a single common bond. In her essay, Irene Dicks-Pearcey wrote:

> Life on Tide's Point was a family commitment. We had a farm on which we kept horses, cows, goats and sheep. Everyone helped in one way or other to care for the animals.

Ironically, perhaps, the very things that urban people often shun are what most children of lighthouse keepers remember as giving them great pleasure. As Irene remembers it, the hour–long walk to and from school in Fox Cove four miles away was carefree, and caring for animals never seemed like work. "We never considered those chores as arduous tasks," she says. As she wrote in her essay, work was fun:

Tide's Point

Those chores provided us children with a great deal of pleasure, especially when a new arrival came to the farm. A name was selected — mostly, a young calf was named after a month in the year, usually the month of birth. A team effort was in place when the time came to cut the hay and stack it away in the barn for feed for the cattle in winter.

During spring, summer and autumn, the entire family participated in getting the gardens ready for planting all kinds of vegetables for the following winter.

The strong sense of togetherness growing up in such remote settings meant that every family member was in tune with the others at all times. As Irene pointed out in her essay, girls were expected to do their share of the hard outdoor work the same as boys. The "total family commitment" as Irene called it, also meant that girls developed many of the same survival skills as their brothers. Irene illustrated a classic example of lightkeeper intuitiveness at a very young age. Her keen sense of observation and quick thinking have been credited with saving the lives of five men.

On Thursday evening, November 13, 1941, eight-year-old Irene Dicks was playing outdoors near the lighthouse on Tide's Point while she waited for her mother to call her in to supper. Irene was always intrigued by fog banks as they developed over the ocean off Tide's Point. As she kept an eye on one fog bank rolling in over Placentia Bay that autumn evening, Irene thought she saw something odd through the dark grey fog. With just a glimmer of daylight remaining in the November late afternoon, the young girl could see what appeared to be the shape of a small boat. Standing at the tip of the 110-foot Tide's Point cliff, Irene strained to get a better look at the object as it drifted slowly toward land. Keeping her eyes trained on the boat, Irene was startled when a brilliant light suddenly illuminated the sky just above the small vessel. Sensing that something was terribly wrong, Irene ran into the house to inform her father that she had seen a boat drifting through the fog, and that a strange light was bursting in the sky just off the point.

Unlike some parents who might have stopped to wonder if such an outburst might have been the work of an overactive imagination, John Dicks didn't hesitate a moment to accept his daughter's account. Running outside, he soon realized that the boat Irene had seen was a lifeboat with five people onboard. The bright light his daughter had described was a distress flare.

Shouting and signalling to the people to direct their vessel to Tide's Cove just north of the lighthouse, John ran to enlist the help of assistant lightkeeper Billy-Joe Power. By the time the lightkeepers reached the beach in Tide's Cove, the boat was already grounded on the rocks. Nearing the shoreline, John and Billy-Joe were shocked to see the five men in the lifeboat had barely enough strength to move.

As they lifted the five from the boat to the beach, John Dicks and Billy-Joe Power were informed that the men were survivors of the SS *Larpool*, a British ship that had been torpedoed by a German U-boat 250 miles off Cape Race. The 6000-ton merchant vessel had left

Halifax in late October with a cargo of tanks, trucks and airplane parts bound for England. At 5:25 a.m. on Sunday, November 2, Commander Alfred Schlieper onboard the German submarine # *208* upped periscope 250 miles east-southeast of Cape Race and fixed the *Larpool* directly in his sights.

The first torpedo was a direct hit. After the surviving British crewmembers had scrambled over the ship's side to the safety of a lifeboat, they watched as a second torpedo cut their ship in half, sinking it rapidly to the bottom.

The captain and four crewmembers from the *Larpool* started toward the coast of Newfoundland hoping to land at Cape Race or Cape Pine. The combination of winds, tides, fogs and currents carried them past their intended destination, all the way into Placentia Bay. Amazingly, after eleven days adrift in a small open lifeboat, all five men were still alive when young Irene Dicks spotted them through the fog bank that evening

Dehydrated, hungry and severely weakened, the survivors needed immediate medical attention. The nearest hospital was only eight miles away but the lightkeepers knew that getting them there would be a challenge. In 1941 there was only a footpath to the main road, a mile from the lighthouse. Slowly John Dicks walked the weakest three survivors up the hill and along the point to where his 1940 Chevrolet was parked just off the main road to Burin. After taking the three men to Fox Cove, John Kavanagh took them to the Burin Cottage Hospital, allowing the lightkeeper to return as quickly as he could to get the other two survivors waiting under the care of Billy-Joe Power.

All five British men survived that ordeal although several of them required care for two months before being released from hospital in Burin.

Grateful to Irene Dicks, the captain of the *Larpool* gave her a first aid kit they had managed to grab before abandoning ship. It was the only thing he had to give as an acknowledgment of the crew's appreciation for her quick thinking and instant response to their plight. Irene (Dicks) Pearcey still has the scissors from that kit in her home in St. John's.

Who Will Rescue the Lightkeeper?

Rescuing fishermen from swamped vessels and hauling sailors from shipwrecks was almost routine activity for lightkeepers. But when lightkeepers run into trouble there was often no one there to help. That's what happened to Edmund Antle in 1972.

Like most men in his area, the fifty-nine-year-old assistant light-keeper loved hunting saltwater birds. Around 5:00 p.m. on April 2, Edmund decided to try his luck at duck hunting. He did well, shooting several birds just north of Tide's Point. When the birds landed in the water, Edmund launched his small dory to retrieve them. His sixteen-year old son, also named Edmund, and his twenty-four-year-old son-in-law Raymond Mullett, were with the light-keeper that evening but they decided to stay ashore. There was a fairly brisk wind outside Tide's Cove Point where the birds had fallen to the ocean. Although the seas were not heavy, Raymond and Edmund Jr. reasoned that it might be a bit risky if three of them crowded into the small dory; they agreed that it would be best if Edmund Sr. went by himself. From the beach, the two young men watched as the assistant lightkeeper rowed his dory out around the point into Herring Cove where the downed birds had drifted.

After waiting for about half an hour, Edmund Jr. and Raymond were getting concerned. Edmund Sr. should have been on his way back by then, they thought, but there was still no sign of the small dory coming around the point. Thinking that Edmund might have spotted more birds, the two young men decided to go to the top of hill to see what he was doing. To their horror, all they could see was the bottom of Edmund's capsized dory. There was no sign of Ed-mund.

After a quick search from the shoreline turned up nothing, Raymond and Edmund Jr. knew they needed help. They needed someone with a boat to search for Edmund Sr. Running to the lighthouse to get a vehicle, the two raced to nearby Fox Cove where they called for help.

Although RCMP officers from Burin, assisted by local fishermen and others, searched the area, it took two days before Edmund's body was recovered.

Without a witness to the event, no one knows exactly what happened. Edmund's widow, Theresa Antle, says that most people think the dory capsized when Edmund was leaning over the side, retrieving the birds. "They think a wave struck the upturned side, tipping the boat over, throwing him into the water," she says. Edmund, who was not wearing any flotation gear, didn't stand much of a chance. Unable to swim and with no one to assist him, it was nearly impossible for the lighthouse keeper to climb to safety on top of the slippery bottom of the overturned dory.

Chapter Ten

Isle of Demons

Belle Isle

The King of Portugal named it Isle of Bad Fortune. He was angry because he believed one of his ships was lost there in 1503, leaving all on board to perish in freezing Atlantic waters. Although not exactly a complimentary title, imagine what earlier mariners thought when they nicknamed it Isle of Demons. But times change and in more recent years, a more genteel and kindly soul renamed it Belle Isle.

French for beautiful island, Belle Isle is situated fourteen miles northeast of the northern tip of the island of Newfoundland at the entrance to the waterway known as the Strait of Belle Isle. The Straits, as its known locally, was recognized by early European explorers as the northern gateway from the Atlantic Ocean to the Gulf of St. Lawrence and subsequently to what is now eastern Canada. French explorer Jacques Cartier passed through the Straits in the spring of 1534. In his journal, Cartier wrote disparagingly about the area: "...there are stones and rocks, frightful and rough. I believe this is the land God gave to Cain."

Twelve miles long by two miles at it widest point, Belle Isle is a stretch of rocky barrens that supports neither trees nor grass. Occasionally though, a daring animal makes it to the island from northern Newfoundland or Labrador on ice floes. One lightkeeper saw the remains of a caribou once, and foxes have managed to survive a few years there from time to time. Polar bears are frequent visitors in winter. The large northern animals spend much of their time on ice floes in the northwest Atlantic in spring and winter, and from time to time they decide to check out Belle Isle. Legend has it that a worker was attacked by a polar bear during the construction of the island's first light in 1858. The story has a happy ending though. When the other workers saw the bear chasing their colleague, they pelted the animal with rocks until, frightened, it scampered away. Alice Roberts, wife of Fred Roberts, a lightkeeper on Belle Isle in the 1950s and 1960s, looked out her kitchen window one evening and was surprised to see a large polar bear staring back at her. Her husband took care of that one with his rifle.

Looking northeastward from the tip of the northern peninsula of Newfoundland, the Isle of Demons/Isle of Bad Fortune rears menacingly out of the sea where the ocean meets the sky. Rising directly up out of the water to over 600 feet in places, the big rocky island intimidates even the most fearless among mariners. Often shrouded in thick fog, the Isle is never to be taken lightly. Even with today's modern navigational technology, one incorrect calculation on a ship's bridge could be the last one.

It is believed that the first French woman to set foot in Newfoundland landed on Belle Isle. Legend has it that Marguerite de la Roche was put off a ship on Belle Isle in 1542 while travelling with her uncle, Jean Francois de la Rocque, Sieur de Roberval. When the French official learned his niece was "misbehaving" with a young man on board the ship, he became enraged and had them both landed on Belle Isle. Marguerite's lover is said to have gone insane on the Isle of Demons and died there, but she survived and was rescued by French fishermen.

The barren island claimed so many casualties that the French government decided to try and help matters in the middle of the nineteenth century. In 1867 the steamer *Napoleon*, which visited Belle Isle in the spring and fall every year to bring supplies to the lighthouse keepers, brought ten men and materials to construct a building to house shipwrecked people.

Despite its size, there are no beaches on Belle Isle, which means there is nowhere to secure anchorage or take refuge from the seas when it's stormy. Newfoundland schooner fishermen sometimes managed to secure ringbolts in the cliffs and by running ropes

Courtesy Ted Warren Navigator Magazine

Lighthouse on Belle Isle Northwest

Belle Isle lighthouse on southwest end of the island. Note small light at the lower part of the cliff.

through the rings, they were able to use the island as anchorage and as a shelter on the leeward side during storms.

No one knows exactly how many ships and souls have been lost to the ravages of Belle Isle's unforgiving cliffs. In 1902, seven New-foundland vessels that had fished in waters surrounding Belle Isle all summer were lost in a vicious storm. Unbelievably, no lives were lost when the ships sank, but their catches of fish along with the remainder of their cargoes were all destroyed.

There are three navigational lights on the island today. Two of them are on the southwest corner. The first light on that end of the island was established on the summit of the cliff in 1858, but mariners complained the light was too high and often impossible to see because of dense fog. A second light was established further down the cliff, closer to sea level. Most often, only one or the other can be seen. A third light, originally built in 1905 – 1906, is located on the island's northeast end.

Wireless operator Jim Kelland on top of the small lower light on Southwest Belle Isle, 1950.

The Accident

Lighthouse keepers and their families are no strangers to tragedy. Most of them have witnessed ships foundering in storms or have been in radio contact with people involved in the unfolding tragedy of marine disasters. Considering the extraordinarily harsh environment where lighthouses are located, there have been surprisingly few accidental deaths of lightkeepers or their families. Belle Isle, however, true to its demonic nickname, claimed the lives of three lightkeepers and one lightkeepers' wife in the worst accident involving lighthouse people in Newfoundland's history. Ironically, *the accident*, as everyone calls it, happened in ideal weather conditions.

Thursday, January 9, 1964 was a fine winter's day in northern

Newfoundland. Twenty-two-year-old Gladys Flynn was keeping a close watch on the weather from St. Anthony that day. Gladys, wife of Clarus Flynn and sister to Henry Fowler, both assistant lightkeepers on the northeast end of Belle Isle, had developed complications during a pregnancy in November, 1963 and had to be taken to hospital in St. Anthony. While in hospital, Gladys suffered a miscarriage. On the advice of her doctor she went to her parents' home in Capstan Island, Labrador for a six-week recovery period.

Because of the difficulty in getting on and off Belle Isle, especially in winter, her doctor insisted on seeing Gladys again before she went back to live in the remote lightstation. After getting the all-clear from her doctor, Gladys waited for the first chance to get to

Gladys Flynn

the island. She knew that a mail plane routinely went to Belle Isle in winter and landed on a frozen pond near the lighthouse on the southwest end. She also knew the pilot would take a passenger or two if there was room.

Things went well that day. Gladys was informed there was room on the plane and she was delighted to learn that her friend Fred Roberts, the principal lightkeeper on the southwest end of Belle Isle, would also be onboard, heading back to work after a few days away.

The ski-equipped plane landed on the pond near the lighthouse without incident. Gladys was taken to the lightkeeper's residence where she was given a meal while Fred Roberts radioed her husband

Clarus at the other end of Belle Isle to inform him that his wife had arrived safely on the island.

While Gladys waited for Fred to return from the marine radio station with news of Clarus, she chatted with Fred's son, Frank Roberts, and his friend Fred Slade, both assistant lightkeepers. Frank and Fred had some good news for Gladys. They told her that Cecil Wellman was on the southwest corner of the island at that very moment and he planned to go home that evening. If that was the case, Gladys might be able to get home sooner than she expected. Cecil was principal lightkeeper on the northeast light where her husband and brother worked. Cecil had come up the day before to visit with his colleagues, a common practice on the island, especially in winter after shipping was brought to a standstill by heavy ice in the Straits of Belle Isle.

Gladys' luck was holding. Cecil Wellman had brought his snow-mobile and a sleigh known locally as a komatik. The snowmobile was a small recreational machine with a gas engine at the back and a single three-foot seat, big enough for two people to sit on. In winter, Cecil often used his snowmobile to tow a komatik, especially when travelling to the lightstation on the southwest corner to pick up mail and supplies.

The prospect of getting home that night became even brighter for Gladys when Fred and Frank mentioned that Cecil had also brought his snow coach, an open box measuring approximately five feet long by two and a half feet wide. The snow coach was lashed to the komatik and used to store supplies when travelling over the barrens. Cecil had also brought his team of huskies with him. The dogs were working animals, usually harnessed to tow a komatik, but on this trip, Cecil just brought them along because they needed a good run.

Around four o'clock in the afternoon, Cecil dropped by the residence where he met Gladys. With Fred and Frank nearby, Cecil and Gladys discussed a possible trip across the island. Although the weather was still clear, they wondered if they should wait until morning since it was getting dark and the trip would take several hours. That's when Frank Roberts and Fred Slade announced that they would also like to go to the northeast end of the island.

L-R Mabel (Wellman) Flynn, Ward Wellman (son of Cecil and Mabel Wellman) and Clarus Flynn.

Fred, aged twenty-three, and Frank, twenty-one, were both engaged to be married later that year — Frank, to a woman from Brador in Quebec and Fred to a woman from Pilley's Island, near his home town of Triton in Notre Dame Bay. Both young men were eager to discuss their wedding plans with as many people as they could. They were especially interested in the advice of women. On an island populated only by lightkeepers and marine radio operators, there weren't many women to talk to. Fred and Frank figured that they could talk to Gladys. They also knew that if they went to the northeast lightstation with Cecil and Gladys, they could tap the knowledge of Shirley Fowler, wife of Henry Fowler, and Cecil's wife, Mabel Wellman.

As Gladys was anxious to get back home and see her husband, it was finally agreed that on such a clear evening with no bad weather expected, there shouldn't be any problems. Cecil Wellman, aged thirty-eight, had worked and lived on the island for years and knew the twelve-mile path very well. Everyone agreed there was nothing to worry about. If they had a problem with the snowmobile, Fred and Frank would help take care of it. Besides, as Cecil suggested, they could harness the dogs if they needed a backup system.

It was a go. Gladys donned Fred Slade's heavy-duty Department of Transport parka and snow pants over her clothing to keep warm. Belle Isle

Cecil Wellman, Frank Roberts and Fred Slade

weather can get extremely bitter at night in the dead of winter. As Gladys climbed into the coach box, Fred sat on the snowmobile behind Cecil. Frank stood on the komatik behind the coach box. Off they went with the dogs running excitedly alongside.

As soon as the four left, Frank's father, Fred Roberts, radioed the northeast lighthouse to inform everyone that they should expect company in a few hours. Gladys' husband Clarus received the message and immediately informed Cecil's wife Mabel and her two children, Dale and Cheryl, that Cecil was on the way. Clarus then relayed the news to his brother-in-law Henry, his wife Shirley and their daughter Patsy.

By eight o'clock, Clarus was getting fidgety. More than three hours had gone by since the group had left the southwest lighthouse and he thought they should be home by now. With two people seated on the snowmobile and towing two others on the komatik, it would take longer than usual, but still there should be some sign of his wife and the others soon. Around 8:30 p.m. Clarus walked up on the hill near the lighthouse to see if there was any sign of the travellers. It was a clear moonlit night and Clarus had no trouble finding his way along the path. He didn't see anyone but suddenly felt a tremendous sense of relief when he heard dogs barking in the distance. Knowing they were Cecil's dogs, Clarus expected to see the group coming down the valley any moment. But relief turned to disappointment within minutes. The dogs were alone.

Although disheartened, Clarus was not entirely surprised to see the dogs without Cecil and the others. Thinking the snowmobile might have been too slow to satisfy the racing dogs, he thought the animals had run on ahead. The dogs had followed the same path from the other end of the island dozens of times; it was not surprising they knew the way home on their own.

With the dogs' arrival, Clarus wondered if the snowmobile had broken down. Taking the dogs with him, he continued walking, hoping to hear or see the group any minute. After walking about two and a half miles, Clarus found fresh snowmobile tracks in the snow. Feeling a great sense of relief at first, he then noticed something that struck him as strange. The tracks were not headed in the direction that he thought they should have been going. Instead of following the usual easterly route, the tracks turned and were heading toward the north side of the island. As Clarus followed the tracks, the dogs became agitated and started to behave strangely, as if scared. He made them follow for a few minutes but then realized he might be wasting time. He thought he might have passed south of the group, since they obviously had taken the northern path. It was likely that the four of them were already safe at home at the lightstation.

Feeling relieved, Clarus turned around and headed back home the same way he had come. His feeling of comfort was short-lived. Arriving at the residence around eleven o'clock, he saw no sign of the snowmobile or the komatik. Gladys and the others were not there.

Considering the possibilities of what might have happened to the group, Clarus explained to Henry, who was new to the island, that although the northern route was a wider path, it was rocky and more exposed. After discussing the situation for a few minutes, they figured the snowmobile had either broken down or was unable to traverse the rocks, meaning the group would have to walk.

Confident that they had figured out the reason for the delay, Clarus and Henry decided they would take the dogs and go and look for the group. Mabel and Shirley packed a few things for the men to take with them. Mabel even put in some brandy for Gladys, thinking the young woman might need something to keep her warm. More than seven hours had passed since they had left, and the temperature had fallen to -15° Celsius.

After they wound the lighthouse clock to keep the light rotating, Clarus and Henry set out again just after midnight, this time with the dogs on a leash. Picking up the snowmobile tracks again, they had no trouble tracing the steps of the group. "At one point we could see where the snow machine had been stuck in the snow and ice because we saw lots of footprints where the men obviously pushed the machine to better conditions," Henry said.

With each step further north, Clarus became more worried and the dogs became more agitated. When they finally reached a small pond, they lost sight of the tracks. The pond ice was covered with snow packed so hard the tracks of the snowmobile were no longer visible. In a strange way, Clarus was almost relieved that he could no longer see tracks. Looking around the pond, he thought this would surely be the place where Cecil, or whoever was driving, would realize that they couldn't continue north much further before they reached the dangerous cliffs on the north side of the island. This, he thought, is where the tracks would turn and go east in the direction of the lighthouse. But after searching the eastern exits from the pond, there were no tracks to be found. A short walk to the left showed the tracks still clearly going north.

Clarus became intensely worried. Having been on that section of the island many times, he knew that just a short distance further in the direction of the tracks, disaster was imminent. That was exactly where the cliff abruptly ended at one of the highest points on the island. Nothing but large jagged rocks and ice lay at the bottom of the cliff, straight down at a ninety-degree angle, nearly 600 feet below.

As the anxiety levels of the lightkeepers heightened, the dogs seemed to sense something amiss also. At first the men thought the dogs were acting strangely simply because they were not on their familiar path between the northeast and southwest ends of the island. But now the four part-huskies were extremely nervous, as if afraid to go a single step further.

Still controlled, but becoming extremely anxious, Clarus asked Henry to stay with the dogs while he went up to the top of a nearby hill and fired shots from his rifle. Hoping that Cecil and the others would hear the gunfire and send back some kind of signal, Clarus fired several shots, listening between each round for a response. One shot produced a brief moment of hope.

"I realize now it was wishful thinking, but I swear I heard someone call out after Clarus fired the gun," Henry says. "I was so sure of it, I even pointed in the direction I heard the voice."

"They're out there," he shouted, pointing in the northerly direction they had last seen the snowmobile tracks heading.

Picking up the tracks again with the assistance of a flashlight, the searchers headed across another small pond, then moved slowly toward the edge of the island. By now, the dogs were extremely agitated and flatly refused to move an inch further. Not wanting to force them any more, Clarus let them go. Within seconds the huskies were hightailing it in the direction of the lighthouse as fast as they could run.

With the dogs gone, an eerie silence descended on the searchers. Moving cautiously toward the edge of the cliff, without speaking, Clarus and Henry knew that hope was growing dimmer with every step they took. As their hearts pounded in their chests, the awful truth became evident. The tracks went straight to the edge of the cliff. There were even boot marks scuffed in the snow over the last few feet to the edge. It appeared that someone, perhaps on the back of the komatik, had seen what was happening and had tried to restrain the sleigh and snowmobile.

Clarus, who had not spoken for a long time, knew the cliff. He turned to Henry and acknowledged there was no hope of finding anyone alive.

Stunned, they stood and stared at the edge of the cliff as if frozen, speechless and barely able to move.

Finally, they started the long journey back to the lighthouse, more than three miles away. Trudging along, dazed, they suddenly noticed footprints in the snow. For a moment their spirits soared. They both thought the four had managed to jump from the snowmobile before going over the cliff and were walking ahead of them.

Their elation was momentary. They soon realized the footprints were their own tracks from a little while earlier.

Both men were in a state of shock and overwhelmed with grief.

Clarus knew the island like the back of his hand and ordinarily would have no trouble finding the way back to the lightstation. But now, confused, he was no longer sure where they were or which way to go. It was only when they saw the red light from Camp Island lighthouse on the Labrador coast that they got their bearings again. Even then it took some time to figure things out. Wondering whether the light was on Camp Island or Cape Bauld, they finally remembered that the Camp Island light was the only red light on the coast.

As if in a trance, the two men walked across the frozen snow.

At approximately 4 a.m., they walked slowly down the hill to the lighthouse residence, wondering how to tell Mabel and Shirley the tragic news. They didn't have to say much. The two women were anxiously staring out the window, hoping to see six people coming over the hill. When they saw only two, they knew something had gone wrong.

"I could tell by the way they were walking that something terrible had happened," Mabel recalls. "They were walking slowly, lifeless, as if they were in a trance."

From the window Mabel and Shirley could see the men as clearly as if it were daylight. The light from the tower had just stopped revolving and was shining directly at them on top of the hill. No one had wound the clock since the two men had left shortly after midnight, meaning that nearly four hours had passed since then. "That's how we know the approximate time we arrived back at the residence," Clarus said. "The light rotated for more than three hours with one winding and it had stopped turning just as we came down the hill."

After spending some time with the women and children, Clarus radioed the marine operator on the southwest end of the island with the bad news. The operator, in turn, notified the RCMP in St. Anthony.

With no time to indulge their own grief, Clarus and Henry started planning the gruesome task of searching for the bodies. The only way to get to the shoreline at the bottom of the cliff where the bodies were located was by boat. Both men knew that heavy ice on the north side of the island might give them serious problems. If winds and tides had packed the ice too tightly against the shoreline, they wouldn't be able to get through.

Daylight confirmed their fears. A quick view from the hill showed that ice had indeed choked the shoreline and there was nothing they could do but wait and hope for a change in wind direction to move the ice offshore.

While they were having breakfast, the wind suddenly chopped around to a fairly strong southeasterly, exactly what they wanted. Immediately after they finished eating, Henry and Clarus hurried to the boat landing to prepare for the three-mile trip. While running the small five and one-half horsepower motor to make sure it was working properly, they loaded their twelve-foot flat-bottomed boat with blankets, clothes, food and whatever they thought they might need, including a cod jigger in case a body had fallen in the water.

The southeast wind had moved the ice far enough offshore for them to make their way through small leads of open water. Although conditions had improved, the going was still tedious because heavy chunks of ice along the shoreline, known locally as ballycatters, were breaking off and moving quickly in the tide toward them. Constantly dodging the drifting ballycatters, they finally made it far enough to see the area where the snowmobile had gone over the cliff.

Heavy ice, rafted several hundred feet from shore, prevented them from getting the boat all the way to the bottom of the cliff. Having no other choice, they hauled the boat up on the ice and walked the remainder of the distance to the shoreline.

Within a few minutes, they spotted the first body lying face-down on a ballycater rafted up on a rocky ledge several feet above sea level. As they got nearer, they noticed a second body, also face-down on the ice, so close to the first one that, for a moment, Henry thought it was just one person. The pair were Cecil Wellman and Fred Slade. A few minutes later, Clarus spotted the bodies of Frank and Gladys out on the ice, several hundred feet from shore.

Realizing that wind and tides could change any minute, pushing the ice further offshore, they knew it was important to retrieve those two bodies as quickly as possible. Emotions ran deep as Henry and Clarus started out on the ice to where Gladys and Frank were. Henry wondered how he would feel when he had to carry his sister's body. At the same time, Clarus was preparing himself to deal with seeing his wife for the first time in two months. Saying nothing, but knowing exactly what had to be done, the men moved the two bodies to a safe resting-place onshore while they discussed their next move.

As they considered their options, they heard a plane fly over the island. The sound of the Labrador Airways Otter lifted their spirits slightly; they knew from a radio message earlier that morning that help, including RCMP officers, was on the way. Because they couldn't get the boat near the bodies, Clarus and Henry decided to leave them and go back to the lighthouse to see if there were Mounties on the plane to help them. Although it was snowing, it wasn't yet bad enough to prevent the experienced pilot from landing on Batteau Pond, about two miles away from the lighthouse. In fact, by the time Henry and Clarus returned to the lighthouse, a second plane was coming. It was Reverend Carl Major, the Anglican Minister from Mary's Harbour, Labrador. Reverend Major piloted his own ski-equipped plane between his various parishes on the Labrador coast.

The Labrador Airways plane had five people on board. Besides the pilot and plane mechanic, there were two RCMP officers and a doctor. They had barely made it in time. While they unloaded supplies, including a snowmobile and stretcher, the weather deteriorated. To make matters worse the RCMP snowmobile broke down; they had to walk to the lighthouse.

Despite worsening weather, everyone agreed they should attempt to get the bodies back to the lightstation as quickly as possible. With the addition of the RCMP officers and the doctor, Henry and Clarus suddenly realized they needed another boat. The small open boat they had used earlier couldn't carry five people in addition to four bodies on the return trip.

There was a small narrow rowboat known as a "rodney" stored behind the lighthouse shed and despite it's unsuitability for such a job, it was the only other boat available. Henry took the doctor, a small man, in the rodney while the two Mounties climbed onboard the other boat with Clarus.

Because the Mounties had to leave the stretcher back with the snowmobile, they were forced to substitute two handbarrows, or handbars, to bring the bodies to the boats.

Once the handbars were onboard, the five men left to get the bodies. The ice conditions hadn't changed; again they were forced to haul the boats up on the ice and walk. Clarus stayed with the boats because winds were increasing and visibility was reduced in blowing snow. The boats needed securing, and if visibility was reducedmuch further, the others might need voice contact to find their way back.

Moments after arriving at the site, the Mounties started to pick up luggage and broken parts of the komatik. Watching with increasing frustration, Henry felt this was no time to start a police investigation. With a storm threatening, he felt the Mounties should wait to do that later. Careful not to offend the officers, Henry said they should start getting the bodies to the boats as quickly as possible. "I don't want to boss you around but the weather is getting worse and we don't have a lot of time before darkness sets in and I guarantee you that you don't want to be out here in a storm after dark."

Agreeing with Henry, the doctor suggested to the RCMP that there would be time to investigate later. Everyone then turned their attention to getting the bodies from the ballycatters and back to the boats.

With the storm worsening, it was getting difficult to see what they were doing. The snow was already so heavy they had lost sight of Clarus waiting at the boats. Henry's biggest concern was the Mounties' inexperience in working on ice floes. With heavy flurries driven by brisk winds, it was easy to mistake snow-covered water between floes for ice. Henry knew that one wrong step could mean death in the freezing waters. Imploring everyone to stay close together, Henry, with help from the Mounties, managed to move the bodies from behind the ballycatters and place them in position to take them to the boats. Henry and one Mountie started walking toward the boats with the heaviest body. The doctor and the other officer placed a second body on their handbar. They had barely started walking when Henry noticed the doctor was having trouble lifting the weight so he suggested that all four take a handle each and carry one body at a time. This worked for a while, but within minutes the doctor was struggling again. Henry took both handles and asked the doctor to guide them through the storm. Still unable to see Clarus, they shouted to see if he could hear them. Luckily, he did and shouted back directions.

By the time they had carried the second body to the boats, the storm had worsened. One of the Mounties suggested they should take the two bodies they had recovered and come back and get the others when the storm abated.

Henry knew the Mountie was making sense but there was no way he could agree. Laying down the handbar, he told the Mounties to continue carrying the body to the boat themselves.

"Where are you going?" they asked.

"You're almost to the boats — I'm going back to get my sister," Henry said, already on his way.

"You can't do that," shouted the Mountie, but his command fell on deaf ears — Henry was already out of sight in the drifting snow.

Twenty minutes later, the policeman was amazed to see Henry struggling through the blowing snow, his sister's body in his arms. "You must be a strong man Henry," the Mountie said.

"I don't know about that sir," Henry replied "but under conditions like this you don't know your own strength and you don't know what you can do."

By now the storm was raging. Although a Mountie had earlier suggested they should go back to the lighthouse, Clarus and Henry realized that if they left then, it could be days before they could get back. Fearing a wind shift would carry the last body out to sea, the lightkeepers agreed that someone had to try to get the body of Fred Slade. The Mounties agreed to go with Henry and although it was a difficult task, they finally managed to beat their way through the storm and get the body back to the boat.

Placing two bodies in each of the boats, the rescuers planned their strategy to get back through the ice floes to the lighthouse. They now had more than ice to worry about — the wind was whipping snow against their faces so fiercely they were nearly blinded. For the first time during the ordeal, Henry felt afraid. "I remember thinking that the boats were severely overloaded and, if we swamped, no one would ever be able to find any of us," he says.

Back at the lightstation, the families, along with the pilot, the plane's mechanic and Reverend Major, were growing increasingly uneasy. Unable to contain her anxiety any longer, Mabel Wellman dressed to go outside. "I'm going to the landing dock to see if there is any sign of them," she said. The minister decided to accompany the distraught woman, but to their dismay the storm was so intense they couldn't see more than a few feet in front of them. The howling winds meant they couldn't hear anything either. They left the landing less than five minutes before the rescuers rounded the Point.

Although winds were very high, the heavy ice floes surrounding the boats created a windbreak and, despite the weather, the small leads of open water were calm. Not taking any chances, the group slowly pushed the boats through the storm until they finally reached the landing dock.

Tired and weak from extremely hard work and weary from too many emotionally charged, sleepless hours, Clarus and Henry knew there was still more work to do. Securing the boats, Clarus asked Henry to go to the lightstation and get the other men to come and help bring the bodies up the steep hill to a shed near the lighthouse. It was so stormy that Henry didn't see the footprints left in the snow by Mabel Wellman and Reverend Major just minutes before.

Barely able to see the person standing next to them, the men somehow managed to fight the blizzard and pull the bodies, one by one, up over the steep hill. Once they placed the bodies in the shed, Clarus and Henry led the way up to the lighthouse residences where everyone spent the night.

Although the most dangerous work was done, the ordeal was still not over. The storm continued unabated on Friday morning, and while the forecast called for improved conditions, the snow didn't taper off until mid-afternoon. "It wasn't till about four o'clock when the skies cleared enough for a plane to take off and that presented us with another problem," Henry said. The plane was on Batteau Pond about two miles away. Without a snowmobile to transport all the bodies at once, there wouldn't be enough time to get all of them to the plane before darkness fell.

With Clarus, Mabel and her children Dale and Cheryl, also waiting to join their deceased loved ones on the flight, the pilot was anxious to accommodate their wishes. What he needed was a place to land closer to the lighthouse. While the mechanic walked to the plane to prepare it for flying, the pilot noticed a fairly level spot in a valley near the lighthouse where the snow from the morning's storm had drifted away in the strong winds. The old snow underneath appeared frozen and packed hard enough to support the weight of his plane. The pilot's guess was right. A short while later he successfully landed the aircraft in time to get the four bodies and the passengers onboard before dark.

Back at the lighthouse, Shirley Fowler was suddenly overcome with grief and loneliness. When everyone left to walk to the airplane, she was alone with only her young daughter Patsy for company. For the first time in nearly two days, there were no other adults to talk to. "What was bothering me most was not knowing what they were faced with in there on the pond, whether the plane was going to make it or if they could get the bodies onboard," she recalls.

Unable to quell her anxiety, Shirley went to the VHF radio and called her cousin, Bobby Davis, an assistant lightkeeper at Point Amour. Bobby had spent several years as an assistant on Belle Isle and was very familiar with the island. His father was also principal keeper there when Bobby was young. He was able to provide detailed information for Shirley about where her husband and Henry and the others were going. He talked to her for hours, describing how long it would take to walk to the valley and what would happen, assuming the plane could land. Bobby's running commentary and descriptions of what was likely happening with the others was comforting to Shirley. "It was as if I could see what was going on in there and that was a big help for me," she says.

It was after dark when Henry finally made it back to the lightstation. Exhausted but relieved, he told Shirley that the plane had made it off the island just before darkness closed in.

Clarus Flynn, Mabel Wellman and her children arrived home in Labrador later that night. Neither of them returned to work or live on Belle Isle again.

Henry Fowler was made acting principal lightkeeper for the remainder of the winter. However, the accident had such a dramatic impact on him and Shirley, they asked to be transferred as soon as possible. A few months later, Henry started work at Point Amour.

Clarus Flynn never worked as lightkeeper again.

Hot Days of a Northern Winter

Like many other lighthouse keepers, Fred Osbourne is carrying on a family tradition. He grew up in the Cape Ray lighthouse where his father, Hiram, was lightkeeper for many years. His grandfather was also a lightkeeper. Fred had three lightkeeper uncles on his father's side of the family as well as one uncle on his mother's side. He also had an aunt who married a lightkeeper.

Fred started work at the light on the southwest end of Belle Isle on January 1, 1968. After spending four years there, he moved to the lighthouse on the island's northeast end, twelve miles away. He worked there for a further three years.

Fred remembers his first winter on Belle Isle as an "interesting experience." Provisions like food and fuel were delivered by vessel to the island in the fall, and there would be nothing more until navigation opened again the following spring, usually in June. Because they didn't have a freezer, the lightkeepers decided to store their supplies of meat in the lighthouse where there was no heat. That was fine in the cold winter months as long as the meat was frozen but when spring arrived and temperatures sometimes rose above freezing in the day, the meat would thaw. Later, usually the same night, when temperatures dropped, it would freeze again. "It would thaw and the blood would run out and then freeze again and thaw again and more blood would run out until finally there was no more blood left in it. You wanna try and eat that," he laughs, shaking his head, "it was like trying to eat a 100-year-old leather boot." It might not have been the

Hauling supplies from the "landing" to the lighthouse on Belle Isle in June, 1950.

most appetizing food sometimes but Fred says he never suffered from food poisoning.

It had nothing to do with food poisoning but Fred had a close call once while on Southwest Belle Isle. The Coast Guard built a new foghorn building in 1968, and for some strange reason the floor paint frequently blistered and bubbled just months after it was applied. In March, 1969, Fred, along with assistant lightkeeper Abner Budgell and the principal keeper Clifford Flynn, decided they were tired of painting the floor every three or four months and it was time to do the job properly. Thinking they must have been using cheap paint, they bought the best concrete paint they could find. Knowing it was useless to put the good paint on top of the old, they had to strip the old paint first. To help loosen it, they sprinkled diesel oil over the floor. They did that on Friday evening and let the oil work the paint all weekend.

Fred was the first to go to the foghorn building on Monday morning. After scraping the flakes of paint for a few minutes, Fred decided it was too cold to work comfortably. He decided to light the oil stove in the other end of the building. A few minutes later, Abner and Clifford joined him and within an hour or two the scraping was finished. Not wanting to waste time, they decided to expedite matters by sprinkling the floor with gasoline to quick-dry what remained of the old paint and diesel oil.

No one is sure exactly what happened next, but within a few seconds they heard the oil stove in the other room burning an intense fire. Apparently the gas fumes trailed to the drafter in the back of the stovepipe and ignited with the flames in the stove. "There was no sudden explosion, all I heard was a loud roar of burning fire and right away I knew the fire wasn't just in the stove," says Fred. The only thing he can remember after that is turning and seeing flames streaking across the floor toward an open door. Turning while trying to scramble to safety, he slipped on the wet floor and fell.

Before he could move, his pants caught fire, seriously burning his legs. As flames raced up his body, burning his arms, Fred somehow managed to get to his feet and, in his words, "made a bee-line for the door. I don't know where Clifford came from; I was the first one out but just as I slowed down Clifford went flying past me, all afire around his waist."

It was pandemonium for a while. "I yelled and yelled at Clifford to stop running and lie down and roll around in the snow. In fact I had to say some pretty nasty things to him to get his attention but even then he still didn't stop running and in no time he was gone out of sight," Fred laughs.

Preoccupied with Clifford's condition, Fred didn't notice that his own clothing was still on fire. "When I looked down, I realized my pants and shirt were burning around my waist." Beating the flames with his hands, Fred finally extinguished his burning clothes and was about to go look for Clifford. Amazingly, Clifford had somehow put out the fire on his clothes and had already come back without

Fred noticing him. "To this day I don't know where the hell Clifford went, but when I looked up again he was standing there looking at me."

"Where's Abner?" Clifford asked.

Fred said he didn't know; in fact things had been so hectic he just realized he hadn't seen Abner since the fire started.

"Well, we got to go back to the building to see if we can get him," Clifford said.

It was only then that Fred realized how serious his own burns were. "I don't know if I can go back," he said to Clifford, glancing at his right arm.

Today, Fred describes his arm as looking like a chicken leg in a pan of boiling fat. "It was completely shriveled and blistered from the upper arm all the way down to my hand." While his injuries were severe, Fred was lucky it wasn't worse. He and the others observed later that the fire was so intense that a large chunk of lead lying on the ground several feet away from the fog-alarm building had melted in the heat.

Despite his discomfort, Fred's concern for Abner overruled his desire to rest. The two lightkeepers started to make their way back to the foghorn building. To their great relief, they saw Abner walking toward them. Although the last to get out of the building, Abner fared a little better then the other two. "His hair was scorched and he was burnt pretty seriously around the neck and he also needed a few stitches in his head from injuries he got from jumping through the window, but other than that he was in pretty good shape," according to Fred.

The full extent of their burns and injuries were not known until the three went to the lighthouse residence. Abner's wife, Neta, a trained nursing assistant, was able to help her husband and Clifford, but Fred's burns were so severe he couldn't stand the pain of anything touching his skin.

At first, Fred insisted on staying outside in the cold air because the heat indoors was unbearable. Eventually, someone convinced him that if he stayed out in the cold too long, he risked going into shock. Reluctantly, he agreed to go inside. A short while later Wally

McLeod, a marine radio operator on Belle Isle, arrived on the scene with a container of ointment to treat the burns. Fred had managed to get out of his burnt pants but his arms were paining too much to attempt removing his shirt.

Fred kept walking around the room in circles. Walking somehow seemed to ease the pain, probably because of the cooler air moving on his burnt flesh. As Fred walked, Wally tried to apply more ointment during each lap. "Every time I'd come near him, Wally would dab a bit more on my arms and legs, while I'd keep walking as fast as I could to keep the air moving on my skin."

Meanwhile, Cyril Myrick, the radio operator on duty, immediately sent word of the accident to officials in St. John's. Within an hour, Dr. Gordon Thomas from the International Grenfell Association Hospital St. Anthony was on the way to the island in an airplane.

It was not funny at the time, but today Fred laughs at how the communications network exaggerated their conditions. "By the time word had gotten from Belle Isle to St. John's and then back to St. Anthony, they were preparing the priests and ministers to give us our last rites," he jokes.

When the plane arrived, Dr. Thomas was surprised to see all three burn victims ready and able to get on board the aircraft on their own. The stretchers were put back on the plane, and they were soon headed for hospital in St. Anthony.

Fred, who was clothed only in underwear and tee shirt, covered himself with a blanket. He felt fine as long as he was in the cold winter air, but inside the plane he became too warm and decided to drop the blanket from his shoulders to his waist. "When old Thomas looked around and saw me, he practically yelled at me to get that blanket back on as fast as I could — I'll never forget the dirty look he gave me," Fred grins.

As soon s they were on the plane, Dr. Thomas offered Fred a sedative. Fred refused, thinking he might need it later. He was right. "By the time we landed on the pond in St. Anthony, I was in such pain that I was good and ready for something: I think I'll have that needle now, doctor," Fred said.

The thing Fred remembers most about the ambulance ride from

the pond to the St. Anthony hospital was people staring from windows. News had spread quickly about the fire on Belle Isle. And, as often is the case, the gossip links had greatly exaggerated the extent of the lightkeepers' injuries. It seems everyone wanted to get a glimpse of the victims as they were being transported to hospital.

As soon as they arrived, an orderly tried to remove Fred's shirt to prepare him for treatment. Obviously not appropriately trained in dealing with burn victims, he was pulling Fred's shirt over his head. "When he did, of course, it felt like the burnt skin started peeling off with the shirt. Well sir, I let out the big one," Fred laughs.

"What the hells flames are ya trying to do with me; don't pull it; cut the goddamn thing off!"

Dr. Thomas, a religious man, didn't take kindly to Fred's outburst, or his choice of words. Although he gave Fred a hard look, the doctor told the orderly to cut the shirt. He didn't say anything to Fred.

Fred, Abner and Clifford survived the ordeal, although Fred says the treatments were more painful than the burns. Dr. Thomas tried a new system of treatment and, although it was very painful, it worked. "We were the first burn victims ever treated in St. Anthony Hospital that didn't suffer from infection during the recovery stages," Fred says.

There's a lighter side to the otherwise serious story of the fire that injured Abner Budgell, Clifford Flynn and Fred Osbourne in 1969. It was a substantial fire that caused a lot of damage. Windows were blown out of the fog alarm building, caps were melted off radiators on the diesel engines, battery tops were melted and insulation on cables was burnt. The three lightkeepers were concerned about losing their jobs because an investigation would clearly indicate the fire was caused by the gasoline they had spread over the floor to dry the old paint. Although it was a common practice to use gasoline for such purposes, Abner, Fred and Clifford were afraid that Coast Guard brass would accuse them of negligence: grounds for dismissal.

After several worried days waiting for news of their employment status, they discovered there was nothing to worry about after all. Because Coast Guard officials in St. John's originally thought the three lightkeepers might have been in danger of dying, an inspector was dispatched to the scene immediately. In his haste to get to the island, the inspector forgot the camera he always used to take pictures during investigations. During a stop at Gander Airport, he picked up a substitute camera and continued to Belle Isle to carry out his work. He worked diligently for several hours, taking lots of pictures of the building, both inside and out, before heading back to St. John's.

Luck was with the three lightkeepers that day. The camera the inspector picked up in Gander was a viewfinder type, not like his own single-lens reflex camera, which views picture subjects through the lens. Forgetting the difference between the two types of cameras, the investigator didn't remove the lens cap and never had a single picture exposed.

Coast Guard officials decided that since Clifford, Fred and Abner were not in danger of dying, as originally thought, there was no need to send the inspector back right away. By the time he eventually returned to Belle Isle, the three lightkeepers were back to work on the site and had done a wonderful repair job on the burnt area, including a brand new coat of paint on the concrete floor in the foghorn building.

Fasten Your Seat Belts

Getting on and off Belle Isle is always a challenge, even on a fine day. In bad weather, it's nearly impossible. Even today, maintenance crews travelling by helicopter prepare for lengthy stays when they go to repair or upgrade the three lights on the island. Fog can blanket Belle Isle within minutes, grounding them for days. And even if it's not foggy, there is wind, heavy seas or almost always something else to worry about.

Pat (Patricia) Gillard will never forget her arrival on Belle Isle one spring when she went back to spend the summer with her parents, Fred and Ettie Roberts. Like many children of lighthouse keepers, Pat had to leave home to go to school. Her first time away from home, six-year-old Pat spent the winter in Pilleys Island, Notre Dame Bay, where she did first grade. When the school season ended, Pat, accompanied by her mother, took the coastal vessel *Northern Ranger* north to Belle Isle. The two-day boat ride was uneventful until they approached Belle Isle. Strong winds suddenly developed and seas became rough. Because there was no wharf on Belle Isle, freight had to be hoisted over the side of the ship in slings attached to a boom and lowered into an open boat. Passengers climbed over the gunwales and down a rope ladder. For some, the thought of climbing twelve or thirteen feet down a rope ladder over the side of a steel ship was terrifying on the best of days. In rough seas, it was a challenge for even veteran seamen and, at times, impossible.

Bringing the *Ranger* as near as he dared to Belle Isle's treacherous rocks, the captain brought his ship into the wind and dropped anchor while Pat's father, Fred Roberts, tried to manoeuvre his motorboat alongside. Although the ship was relatively stable in the rough seas, the lightkeeper's boat bobbed around like a cork. Pat remembers the boat rising on the crest of the seas, bringing her father almost up to the height of the *Ranger*'s deck. An instant later, he would be twenty feet below in the trough of the waves. Ettie Roberts managed to climb down the ladder and hung on until her husband's boat came close enough for her to jump to safety. The next task was to get Pat from the vessel.

Determined to get his daughter from the ship, Fred Roberts shouted to one of the ship's crew to throw Pat and he would catch her.

"I remember this man, one of the crew, picking me up and carrying me in his arms to the side of the ship. It was horrible. He had all he could do to stand up because of the ship's rolling. They even threw oil over the side of the *Ranger* to smooth the waters but that didn't make much difference," Pat says, shaking her head at the thought of winding up in stormy seas coated in oil. Despite her father's pleas to throw Pat from the ship, the crewman was afraid a sudden unexpected wave might toss the small boat away from the ship and Pat would wind up in the ocean.

Finally after repeated pleas from Fred, the crewman waited in readiness for just the right moment. Watching carefully as Fred's boat rose and fell on the waves, the crewman finally saw an opportunity and flung Pat away from the ship. His calculations were perfect. Fred, sure-footed as a mountain goat, was poised in just the right position to snatch his daughter from the air safely into the small boat.

Being tossed through the air from the safety of a rolling ship in rough seas was an incredibly traumatic experience for a six-year-old girl. For lighthouse keepers like Fred Roberts, that kind of incident was simply the lifestyle in a harsh northern environment.

The Crash

Getting his daughter safely back on Belle Isle was only mildly problematic for Fred Roberts compared to a time several years earlier when he tried to get off the island. As an assistant lightkeeper on Belle Isle in 1946, he learned that sometimes it was more than bad weather that caused trouble.

In July that year, Fred was busy installing a steel pipe in a piece of equipment in the fog alarm building on the southwest end of the island. Suddenly, a sharp piece of steel fell from a shelf, striking Fred's arm. An assistant lightkeeper grabbed the first aid kit and tried to remove a piece of the steel near Fred's elbow. Unfortunately, a small piece of the metal was left inside the flesh and, within days, the arm became severely infected, causing blood poisoning.

After consulting the regular Coast Guard medical advisor, a doctor in New Brunswick, on VHF radio, Fred was told he needed medical treatment at a hospital immediately. When Fred contacted his superiors in St. John's to tell them about his condition, a Catalina Flying Boat was dispatched from Gander the next day to get him.

Although there was a fairly heavy swell on the ocean that day, there were no whitecaps or "breakers," as they are also known locally. The pilot managed to land the large aircraft safely and taxied the plane to a small cove under the cliff, near the lighthouse.

Besides the injured lightkeeper, there were two marine radio operators from Belle Isle waiting to board the flying boat that afternoon. Bobby Davis, an assistant lightkeeper, operated a tractor and a small homemade flatbed trailer constructed from the chassis of a pick-up truck. Bobby hitched the trailer to the tractor and carried the three men and their luggage down the hill to the rocky shoreline. At

Courtesy Canadian Coast Guard, Fisheries and Oceans

Fog alarm, Belle Isle Southwest (circa 1920).

the bottom of the hill, assistant lightkeepers Hedley Buckle and Spofford Earle were waiting with an eighteen-foot dory to take the three men to the flying boat, about a quarter-mile offshore.

Fred and his friends climbed onboard the big airplane and prepared for take off. Everything went according to plan until they got outside the cove. Sizing up the sea conditions, the pilot decided to taxi out around the nearby headland and head into the wind for take-off. After a few minutes riding up and down on the swell, the pilot gave the plane additional throttle to gain enough speed for lift-off. For a few moments the plane skimmed over the tops of the waves like a powerful speedboat. Just as it appeared ready to rise into the air, a huge wave struck the bottom of the flying boat and dragged it crashing back into the water. The jolt was so severe the co-pilot was flung from his seat in the top of the two-story plane, landing on the floor several feet below.

After assurances that neither the co-pilot nor the plane was seriously hurt, the pilot decided to try it again. Turning the aircraft around, he attempted to ride the waves in a slightly different direction. It worked. This time he managed to get up enough speed to ride over the crests of the swell, finally clearing the water and rising into the air. Everything would have been fine if the pilot had only kept flying the Catalina straight ahead a few seconds longer. Thinking he had fully cleared the surface, the pilot banked the plane to the left to head south to St. John's. Unfortunately, he miscalculated his altitude and the height of the seas. When he turned the plane, the left wing dipped too close to the ocean and a float underneath the wing dug into the crest of a rising wave.

Halfway up the hill to the lighthouse, Bobby Davis couldn't believe his eyes. Curious to see how the plane was doing, he turned around just in time to see the flying boat smash into the water about a half-mile from the island. "I couldn't believe it," he says. "That big plane whipped around on the water like it was a spin top before it finally settled into the ocean."

Hedley Buckle and Spofford Earle were almost back to shore in the dory when they heard the plane crash. Knowing the crew and passengers would need help, they leaned on their oars and started rowing back toward the plane as quickly as they could.

Inside the plane, the flight crew was busy assessing damages. At first glance, it looked like a bomb had exploded. Pieces of equipment had been flung through the cabin and cockpit hitting several of the men.

Glancing outside, one of them noticed that the float under the left wing had been totally ripped off the aircraft when it struck the water. Without buoyancy from the float, the tip of the left wing had already submerged and the plane was listing heavily to the left side. Within moments, saltwater came rushing into the aircraft through a door that had popped open when the plane struck the water. A quick assessment of their situation told the five-man crew they needed to get the three passengers and themselves out of the plane immediately.

For a few moments no one was sure how to get out. Finally, someone noticed that the bubble-shaped glass skylight on top of the airplane had broken. It was a tight squeeze but the opening was large enough to crawl through if they could climb up to the area. The marine radio operators made it safely through the top first. Then Fred Roberts ploughed through the rubble from the back of the cabin to look at the escape area. Although handicapped because of his severely weakened arm, Fred somehow managed to pull himself up through the opening and scrambled to join his friends who were huddled on the right wing of the flying boat.

Up front in the cockpit area, four of the flight crew were preparing to head to the skylight when they noticed the fifth flyer lying lifeless on the floor. Only then did they realize that he was unconscious after being thrown violently against the wall during the crash. Despite being submerged in the cold seawater for several minutes, the man finally regained consciousness and, with the help of his fellow crewmembers, slowly started toward safety through the broken window.

By the time all eight men had reached the wing, the airplane was nearly submerged. In their haste to get out, no one had remembered to bring lifejackets from the locker. The experienced flyers knew that, even in summer, the cold water would cause hypothermia in ten or fifteen minutes. A lifejacket would at least help keep their heads above water, giving them extra survival time while they waited for help to arrive.

The crew soon realized that getting the lifejackets was almost impossible. The plane had filled with water on its left side, totally flooding the compartment where the jackets were stored. Because of the debris, the only way to get to that section of the plane was to dive into the ocean and swim into the aircraft through the submerged door. After retrieving the lifejackets, the person would then have to swim back out again underwater. It was an extremely dangerous undertaking but the plane's mechanic said he wanted to attempt it. A strong swimmer, he was also aware that he had received fewer injuries than the others.

As the mechanic dove from the wing, the seven others watched and waited with bated breath, worrying the man might get trapped inside the plane. It was a long couple of minutes, but he finally appeared on the surface carrying two lifejackets. Luckily, water had not filled the plane all the way to the roof where the lifejacket locker was located, allowing the diving mechanic some breathing room inside the aircraft. However, because of the buoyancy of the lifejackets, it was impossible to carry more than two of them underwater at once. Having no choice, the mechanic dived twice more until he became so exhausted he could barely swim.

As it turned out, the diver's heroic efforts were not necessary after all. Spofford and Hedley had already made it to the side of the plane in the dory, ready to begin their rescue mission.

From his vantage point on the island, Bobby Davis was stunned at what he was seeing. The sinking plane reminded him of a huge whale, with its left fin underwater and the right one pointing toward the sky. Spellbound, Bobby watched as the rescuers first pulled the mechanic from the water and got him safely on board the dory. Then they manoeuvred the boat as close to the sinking airplane as possible. The dory was riding up and down on the seas like a piece of flotsam while the half-submerged airplane, by then heavily laden with water, was hardly moving at all. "When the small rescue boat rose up on the swell it would come up under the wing and then one of the guys on top of the wing would make a jump for the boat," Bobby says.

No one missed the dory and ended up in the water, but some of the men hesitated too long before jumping. They jumped when the boat was falling away from them in the trough of the waves, instead of jumping when it was coming closer toward them on the crest. Those men received numerous cuts and bruises when they landed on the bottom of the dory. There were times Bobby wondered if the men might have been better off jumping into the ocean first and then, with the help of those onboard, they could climb into the boat. They might have received fewer injuries that way, he thought.

Finally, as the last man landed safely in the dory, the lightkeepers pulled away from the sinking plane and headed for the beach. They got away just in time according to Bobby. "They were no more than a hundred yards away from the plane when she slid beneath the surface."

Meanwhile, Bobby, who had loaded the trailer with a ton of coal for their stoves that winter, dumped his cargo and started toward the beach with the tractor. Judging by what he had seen, he thought several of the men would have trouble walking up the steep hill to the lighthouse.

When the dory came close enough for Bobby to get a good look at the eight men, he thought all of them would need a ride. 'There was blood everywhere," he says. "It reminded me of times when fishermen would come in with a boat load of seals — the dory looked like it was full of blood."

Besides the beatings they suffered in the crash and the climb through the debris inside the plane, some men received injuries as they crawled through the broken window. Others were injured when they jumped from the wing into the boat. All of them received numerous cuts to their arms and legs. Luckily, their injuries appeared a lot more serious than they actually were. A lot of the cuts were superficial and, although covered in blood, most of the men were in reasonably good shape and were able to walk up the hill without assistance. The mechanic was the only one who couldn't make it on his own. Suffering from the early stages of hypothermia as well as exhaustion, he managed to walk to Bobby's trailer and gratefully accepted a tractor ride up the hill to the lightstation. All eight men were treated for cuts and bruises and were soon on the road to recovery.

The next day, a Canadian Navy corvette patrolling the waters off northern Newfoundland was diverted to Belle Isle to pick up the flight crew, the radio operators and Fred Roberts, taking all eight men to St. John's.

Fred Roberts finally received the treatment he needed for blood poisoning and made a full recovery. A few days later he was back at his post as assistant lightkeeper on Belle Isle.

Chapter Eleven

Island of Cod

Baccalieu

Baccalao — Bacalao — Baccale — Baccaleau —Baccalow — Bacca-laos — Baccalho — Baccalauras. Any of those might have been the original name for what finally became Baccalieu. "Baccalao" is a Portuguese word meaning "cod" while Baccalauras is "island of cod." Because waters surrounding Baccalieu Island have been prized historically as a cod fishing area, scholars are certain the modern spelling is a variation of one of the Portuguese terms.

Ironically, the island with the Portuguese name is perhaps best known for all the British names given to the coves and inlets along its rocky shores. There are places like Falmouth, Plymouth, Bristol, London and Wales. Former Newfoundland Premier Joe Smallwood visited Baccalieu during a political campaign in the 1950s and later joked that he'd had breakfast in London, lunch in Wales and supper in Bristol. Other places on the island have names that conjure up more colourful images. Murdering Hole, Lassie Cove and Pirates Gulch come to mind. It's not known if pirates ever used the island as a landing site, but in 1612 Newfoundland's most famous pirate, Peter Easton, set up operations in Harbour Grace and Brigus, just a few miles from Baccalieu. Many people in Conception Bay believe Easton was a regular visitor to the rocky island.

For hundreds of years, Baccalieu Island was one of the most strategic navigational points in eastern Newfoundland. From the time Europeans started sailing the coastline, the small island, three miles off the tip of Conception Bay, was used as a reference point for mariners to calculate departure and return positions. Located forty miles northwest of St. John's, Baccalieu was even the reference point in one of the province's best known folk songs, "Jack Was Every Inch a Sailor." According to the song, sailor Jack was born on a boat very near St. John's, but there was no mention of Newfoundland's capital city. Instead, the songwriter chose an even better known location to pinpoint Jack's birthplace:

> 'Twas twenty-five or thirty years since Jack first saw the
>   light
> He came into this world one dark and stormy night
> He was born on his father's ship as she was lying to
> 'Bout twenty-five or thirty miles southeast of Baccalieu

As recently as the 1940s and the introduction of sophisticated navigational aids like radar, Newfoundland sealing ships steered northeast into the Atlantic from Baccalieu to get to the ice fields. To get back to port, they would follow the southerly flow of the ice for a day or two and then veer west to seek Baccalieu, their point of departure. When they saw the island, the sealing captains would take their bearings and head for port, usually St. John's, where their seals were sold. Because of Baccalieu's prominent location, a lighthouse was built there in 1858.

Although Baccalieu Island is three miles long and a half mile wide, it wasn't always easy for sailors to find, even with a lighthouse. Often invisible in thick fog or snowstorms, the 450-foot cliffs were always approached with extreme caution.

The Ryans of Baccalieu

James Ryan was Baccalieu's first lightkeeper. Ryan, an Irish immigrant to Newfoundland, worked as a ship's pilot in St. John's. In 1857, Ryan piloted a British ship through the narrows to the safety of the harbour. A high-ranking British government official onboard the ship was impressed with Ryan's abilities and arranged to have him offered the job as lighthouse keeper on Baccalieu Island when the new light went into operation the following year. Ryan accepted the offer and twelve months later, on December 20, 1858, James Ryan and his wife were headed for Baccalieu Island.

A pleasant surprise awaited the Ryans. Unlike most newly constructed buildings, the Baccalieu lighthouse and residence were as tidy as a whistle when they arrived. It seems the government official in charge of start-up operations wanted the Ryans to get off on the right foot in their new endeavours. The government man approached a young woman named Ann Fowlow, who

Courtesy Ryan family

Frank Ryan — lighthouse keeper on Baccalieu Island 1891-1941.

Courtesy Canadian Coast Guard, Fisheries and Oceans

Baccalieu Island.

Baccalieu Island lighthouse and residence — circa 1900.

was living on the island that year with her family, and asked if she would clean the lighthouse and the new residence before the Ryans arrived. In return for her generosity, the man said she would be given the privilege of igniting the first light in the brand new lighthouse, probably the first time in Newfoundland a woman was given that distinction. Ann gratefully accepted the deal. During the official opening ceremonies the next day, Ann proudly took the torch and lit the Baccalieu light for the first time. To her surprise, the dignitaries attending the festivities then pronounced Ann "Queen of Baccalieu."

She didn't know it at the time, but Ann Fowlow would see the lighthouse on Baccalieu many times after that. The "Queen of Baccalieu" met James Ryan's son, John, that day just before Christmas in 1858. Shortly afterwards, Ann Fowlow became Ann Ryan and lived with her husband at the lighthouse when John took over from his father in 1876. Baccalieu was home to Ann (Fowlow) Ryan for the next sixty years.

For nearly a hundred years, the Ryan family kept the light burning on the north end of Baccalieu Island. When John Ryan died in 1891, his twenty-year-old son Frank abandoned his studies at St.

Bon's College in St. John's and began a lightkeeping career that lasted fifty years. When Frank retired in 1941, his eldest son Jim became the last of the Ryans of Baccalieu to take charge of the light. Jim's brother Edmund worked with him as assistant keeper. The Ryan dynasty on Baccalieu Island ended in 1950 when Jim and Edmund quit the lightkeeping business and moved to Ontario.

On Top of the World

Like other lighthouse families, the Ryans of Baccalieu saw their share of adventure. Also, like their colleagues in other places, the surviving Ryans have fond memories of their days living on the island. As far as they were concerned, they were on top of the world.

The abundant marine life around Baccalieu provided more than a food supply for the lightkeepers and their families. The wildlife was also a source of entertainemnt. In spring, the Ryans would walk the cliffs and watch thousands of seals bobbing up and down in Baccalieu Tickle during their annual migration south. In summer, huge whales, chasing capelin and other prey, would venture very close to the rocks.

Although there were no trees on Baccalieu, there were lots of birds. The island was home to tens of thousands of seabirds. Murres, known also as turrs or Baccalieu birds, puffins, seagulls and gannets put on a show all year round. Gannets would soar high above the cliffs and in the blink of any eye, dozens of the large white birds would suddenly slice downward through the air, diving deep into the ocean in pursuit of a fish dinner. As is often the case with people who live close to nature, the same seabirds that provided entertainment for the Ryans also provided them with many dinners. "I remember Mother cooking as many as fifteen puffins for Sunday dinner because we often had visitors joining us on the weekend," John Ryan remembers.

Besides the gift of abundant natural wildlife on Baccalieu, the Ryans also kept cows, hens, goats and other animals. "The animals and birds were my friends," Mary Ryan says.

As in most lighthouses, the Ryans had a wonderful view from atop the cliffs of Baccalieu. Mary Ryan laughs at a story her mother

Courtesy Ryan family

Baby Mary Ryan and her mother,
Charlotte.

always told about a woman from Bay de Verde who visited them one summer. Charlotte Ryan was showing the woman around the lighthouse and, because it was a warm day, Mrs. Ryan took her friend out on the catwalk around the top of the light tower. Admiring the tremendous view of both Conception and Trinity Bays from nearly 500 feet above sea level, the visitor suggested that she would love to have her afternoon tea in the light tower every day. Mrs. Ryan laughed and reminded her friend that there were many days she would not enjoy afternoon tea at the top of the lighthouse, especially in the height of a norwester in February.

For Mary Ryan, the top of the light tower meant more than a good view. She has fond memories of riding on the light. Like many other lights in Newfoundland and Labrador, the Baccalieu light revolved. Similar to a cuckoo clock apparatus, the light was turned by a heavy weight attached to a chain. As the weight slowly sank to the floor of the fifty-foot tower, it activated a series of wheels that in turn rotated the light. Turning all the way around once every minute, the revolving light was the next best thing to having her own personal merry-go-round.

Mary also remembers a different ride — one that she didn't want to try a second time. Looking for something different to do one day, she and her brothers John and Edmund decided they would take a ride in their father's makeshift crane. The crane consisted of a box attached by rope to a boom that swung out over the cliffs. Their father used the motorized crane mostly to hoist provisions such as coal, fish and food supplies from a boat at the foot of the steep cliff. Edmund started the motor while Mary and John got in the small gondola-type box. A few minutes later Edmund and Mary were swinging above the rocky waters of Baccalieu Tickle fifty feet below. It was great fun for a while but when she realized what could happen if the engine failed or if the boom or rope broke, Mary Ryan decided that she'd been Mary Poppins long enough.

Living at nearly 500 feet above sea level, the Ryans enjoyed crystal-clear AM radio reception. When their father Frank purchased a radio in 1936, life for the Ryans changed dramatically. Evenings were filled with hours of newscasts and delightful entertainment. The serial drama ,Irene B. Mellon, on radio station VONF in St. John's was a big hit with Mary. Running from 1934 to 1941, the popular show featured a fictitious Newfoundland schooner with a crew of ten. The crew encountered dramatic adventures in ports all over the world. Mary still has pictures of the cast. John and Edmund were delighted to be able to listen to live hockey broadcasts from Canada, while Frank and Charlotte were faithful listeners to the Gerald S. Doyle News Bulletin, a half hour of news and weather information topped with dozens of personal messages every evening. Other popular local programs enjoyed by the Ryans included the Barrelman with J.R. Smallwood and Uncle Tim's Barndance, which was broadcast live from the Knights of Columbus Hall on Saturday nights.*

Radio reception was so clear on Baccalieu Island that the Ryans became regular listeners to stations in the United States, England, Ireland and even Italy. "I remember listening to Big Slim the Lone Cowboy. He did a country music program on WWVA in Wheeling, West Virginia," Mary says.

"And remember Radio Erin from Ireland and then there was the program from Rome we always listened to as well," John adds.

During the war years, the Doyle Bulletin on VONF was required listening for lighthouse keepers. In the so-called "blackout" times

---

* Ninety-nine people died when the hall caught fire and burned to the ground during the Barndance on December 12, 1942. Two of the victims were radio personnel who were broadcasting the live proceedings at the dance that night.

when lights everywhere had to be extinguished in case of an air raid, lightkeepers were instructed to listen to the Bulletin every evening for a message from the government in St. John's to find out if they should put out the light. Obviously, the enemy would be greatly assisted in locating targets if they could pinpoint the location of a lighthouse. Introduced by the music of a marching band, the announcer would read the introduction to the program in a commanding voice: "Attention all lightkeepers, south and east coast of Newfoundland; Carry out following instructions. The announcer then read the coded message to lightkeepers.

"N for Nuts — A for Apples," Mary says.

"N for Nuts — B for Butter," Edmund pipes up, talking over his sister.

"And N for Nuts and C for Charlie," John chimes in, as all three laugh at the memory. Mary and her two brothers heard the codes so often they can still recite them in their sleep, more than fifty years later.

Although a top secret during the war, the Ryans now explain that NA (N for Nuts — A for Apples) was the code to maintain status quo and leave the light burning. NC (N for Nuts — C for Charlie) meant put out the light and NB (N for Nuts — B for Butter) was the code to start the light again.

Perhaps it was her days listening to radio stations from several countries that raised Mary Ryan's curiosity about people and cultures in other parts of the world. She had often wondered about the different accents she heard on the radio. She was curious about what people in other countries did for a living and what their lives were like. One day, Mary decided to satisfy her curiosity. During her last year on Baccalieu, she wrote letters to two Canadian newspapers asking for pen pals. Fascinated with the idea of a young woman living in a lighthouse on a remote island off the east coast of Newfoundland, thousands of people immediately responded. Letters came from people all across Canada, the United States, Ireland and England. "The poor ferryman — the man who brought the mail across the Tickle — was worn out, bringing all this mail," Mary laughs.

Overwhelmed with the response, Mary replied to as many people as she could, but she simply didn't have time to write all of them.
She deliberately chose not to reply to some of the writers. She
remembers being annoyed with one young man who wrote from
England. "He wanted to know if fish was the only thing we New-
foundlanders ate and he seemed to take pleasure in saying that he
couldn't find much information about Newfoundland. I didn't think
he was very nice so I didn't write him back."

Prayers, Yarns and Secret Stashes

Life was never boring for the Ryan family. Like his father and
grandfather before him, Frank Ryan had a full day's work every day
tending the kerosene-fuelled light. In summer, Frank also tended to
a small sideline business. Baccalieu was a favourite fishing location
for dozens of Trinity Bay fishermen, especially crews from Winterton. Every spring the Winterton men would show up in their small
fishing vessels they called "bully-boats" and set up living quarters
perched on the side of the cliffs. Each summer Frank Ryan purchased
cod livers from the fishermen to render into oil. Between his lightkeeping work and running a small liver oil plant, Frank Ryan didn't

Courtesy Ryan family

Summer fishing stages on Baccalieu Island.

have much time to spare.

But no matter how busy things were, Frank Ryan and his wife Charlotte always made time for "prayers." A devout Roman Catholic, Frank always made sure the family gathered around the dining room every evening to say the rosary. "More Protestants said the rosary at our house than in any other Catholic household in Newfoundland, I'm sure," Mary laughs. In summer it was customary to have friends from the mainland of Newfoundland visit, especially on weekends. If their company included Protestants, Frank always tuned in to the St. John's radio station to listen to Sunday services for them. Afterwards, it was "Catholic Hour" at the lighthouse, when everyone knelt to say the rosary. If they didn't have visitors, Frank Ryan made sure to bundle everyone up and steam six miles in his open boat to attend mass in Bay de Verde. In winter and when bad weather prevented them from going to Bay de Verde on Sunday morning, Frank held his own mass. "We always had to read the mass prayers and then at night, before we had the rosary, we had a sermon book, and father would read the sermon," Mary says.

Lent was a period of intense worship in the Ryan household. "We'd have the rosary at twelve o'clock and at four o'clock it would be the Stations of the Cross, which was twenty minutes and then another rosary and God only knows how many litanies after that," John remembers.

For the young Ryan children, all that worship was a little tedious, especially if someone came to visit while the rosary was being said. "If someone came in halfway through the rosary, father would start the whole thing all over again from the beginning," Edmund says.

John remembers one time when two men from Bay de Verde dropped by during one of the Lenten prayers. They turned up just moments before the ritual was about to end, and one of the men asked if Frank would mind starting again. John, anxious for prayers to conclude in order to get back to the things he wanted to do, was livid. "I felt like choking him," he laughs today.

John, Mary and Edmund are all quick to point out that although their father was a religious man, he wasn't fanatical about it. "He liked his drink too, you know," John says, implying that liking a drink made his father somehow less religious.

"Oh yes, in fact he loved a little drop now and then," Mary is quick to add.

Like many Newfoundland men in those days, Frank liked to stash away a few bottles of moonshine, whisky or rum. There were several reasons for concealing liquor. Usually, it was a matter of rationing supplies to maintain a consistent supply. Newfoundland men have long been recognized as hearty drinkers, and closing time came only when there was nothing left to drink. There had been more than one occasion when Frank Ryan woke up with nothing but empty bottles when friends from nearby communities had visited.

Because there was no corner liquor store to run to and pick up a bottle, replenishing the shelves often took a long time. Frank also liked a straightener some mornings, so he usually kept a spare bottle tucked away for what some would describe as "medicinal purposes."

John remembers one morning when his father was not feeling well. There had been a party the night before and Frank couldn't find anything in the house to ease the pain of his aching head. After watching his father's discomfort for about an hour, John remembered a bottle of shine that had been sitting in the light tower for weeks. Glad to be helpful, he told his father about it. "Oh my God, go get it for me John," Frank said, his eyes brightening at the thought of a "wee one" to set the morning straight. A minute later John handed his father what he thought was a lovely clear bottle of shine. Not stopping to inspect the contents, Frank tipped up the bottle and drank a mouthful of engine oil. "I thought he was going to die," John says, laughing heartily at the memory.

Although he really enjoyed an occasional drink, Frank was not a problem drinker. In fact, John liked to stash away a bottle for his father as a little surprise when the cupboard was empty. One year John decided to put away some whisky for his father for a surprise on St. Patrick's Day. "Dad always like a drink on St. Patrick's Day so for weeks I used to go around and take a little bit of whisky from bottles and pour it into a bottle that I was hiding in my room." Everything was going according to plan until one day Charlotte discovered the bottle hidden in her son's room. After a thorough interrogation about whether John was stealing whisky and secretly drinking it, Charlotte was satisfied that he was doing a good thing and left the bottle with her son.

A few days later Frank came home in the evening tired from a long day hunting seabirds in addition to working the light. "My God, Charlotte, I'm chilled to the bone after all day in an open boat — I'd love to have a little drink to warm me up this evening," he said. Thinking that her husband deserved a bonus after his hard day, Charlotte told Frank about the secret bottle that John had been keeping for St. Patrick's Day. "Well, it wasn't long before he had finished the whole thing," John says. While his father sipped, John explained how he'd been taking a little bit of whisky every time he saw an open bottle, pouring some of it into his own container. Afraid he might get caught, John was careful not to take too much at once. Feeling much warmer after his nice tall drink, Frank looked at his son and then at the empty bottle and playfully admonished the youth. "Why didn't you take out a little more while you were at it?" he laughed.

Like most of his fishermen friends, Frank always enjoyed a glass of whisky when he had visitors. "I loved it when men like Jackie Rice from Red Head Cove and others would come to the island to visit — it was as good as radio," Mary says. "Sometimes, father would play the fiddle and everyone would get up and dance around the kitchen — it was great fun."

The entertainment at the Baccalieu lighthouse wasn't confined to music and dancing. Known as a great storyteller, Frank Ryan could spin a yarn with the best of them. Mary and her three brothers looked forward to evenings when their father had visitors who would sit at the kitchen table and trade stories. Not surprisingly, many of Frank's stories were about shipwrecks near Baccalieu.

One spring in the mid-1860s, a convoy of sealing ships returning from the ice fields didn't find the island until it was too late. Caught in a snowstorm with strong northeasterly winds, the entire fleet got blown ashore and was smashed to pieces as heavy ice pounded against the wooden hulls of the schooners. Fortunately, the sealers were able to get off the ships and walk to the island on the ice pans.

For lightkeeper James Ryan and his wife, the unexpected arrival of 150 sealers was a bit overwhelming. Luckily, the sealers had time to salvage food supplies before abandoning their schooners because it was impossible to get fresh supplies to the island in spring when heavy arctic ice choked Baccalieu Tickle. The Ryans made the sealers as comfortable as possible by spreading blankets and whatever materials they could find over the floors in every room the house. Several men even set up bunks in the lighthouse.

Often an impediment to travelling across the three-mile tickle, the spring ice that year provided a bridge for the 150 sealers. After two days of waiting for the weather to improve, several of the men noticed the ice floes had been packed together tightly enough to walk on. Adept at picking their way through the ice pans as part of their jobs, the sealers left to walk across the tickle. A few hours later all 150 of them were safe in Bay de Verde on the Newfoundland mainland.

Edmund, Jim, Mary and John Ryan often heard their father talk about the mystery surrounding the sinking of the SS *Lion* in 1882. Frank, only ten years old at the time, was one of the first people to discover that the *Lion* had been wrecked.

The 300-ton wooden steamer was well known as a sealing ship. On her first trip to the seal harvest in 1867, the *Lion*, under the command of Captain R. Dawe, was the first steamer to make port that spring carrying a load of nearly 5,500 seal pelts. The rest of the year, the *Lion* was a freighter and passenger ship around the coast of Newfoundland.

Shortly after midnight on January 6, 1882, the *Lion* slipped through the narrows of St. John's Harbour bound for Trinity with nearly thirty passengers and crew and a cargo of sealing supplies. The captain was Patrick Fowlow, a veteran skipper from Bay de Verde whose sister Ann was married to John Ryan, the lighthouse keeper on Baccalieu Island.

Although it was the dead of winter, the weather was nearly perfect — a clear moonlit night with only a gentle breeze blowing from the west. It was such perfect weather that passenger Mrs.

Elizabeth Cross said she might settle down for the night on the deck of the schooner. Mrs. Cross, prone to severe seasickness, knew that she would feel much better on deck than below. Reportedly, the woman found a sheltered place behind a pile of planks and decided to stay there for the journey.

The fine and unusually warm weather held all through Old Christmas Day. A group of children decided to take advantage of the fine day and went to the west side of Baccalieu Island for a picnic. After lunch, some of them went to explore a small inlet called Falmouth Cove. Their exploration turned up more than they expected. Looking toward Baccalieu Tickle, they saw wreckage and a woman's body floating just a few hundred feet from the shoreline. One of the pieces of wreckage was a parcel, addressed to Miss Ryan, Baccalieu. The body was that of Elizabeth Cross.

Nobody knows what happened to SS *Lion*. The schooner's hull was never found and the only body ever recovered was that of Mrs. Cross. No one is even certain where and how the schooner sank. Captain Fowlow had navigated the waters around Trinity and Conception Bays for many years and knew the location of every rock and shoal. It is doubtful the experienced captain would have accidentally steered too close to Baccalieu Island on such a clear night. It appears that whatever happened, the vessel sank to the bottom very quickly — so fast that no one had time to get to a lifeboat. One popular theory is that an explosion caused the sinking, although no one on Baccalieu Island or nearby communities heard or saw anything. The *Lion* was carrying sealing supplies, including several barrels of blasting powder. The reason Mrs. Cross was the only one found might have been that she was the only person on deck.

Speculation about what happened to the SS *Lion* was fodder for lengthy chats at the Baccalieu lighthouse for many years. To this date, there is still no evidence to solve the mystery.

One of Frank Ryan's favourite stories was about the loss of the sealing schooner *Seal*. One morning in April, 1926, Frank noticed what appeared to be smoke on the southeast horizon. After a closer look through his spyglass, he clearly saw heavy smoke billowing from the stern section of a schooner. The lightkeeper had no means of contacting government authorities but as luck would have it, a friend who had stayed on the island overnight with the Ryans was just leaving to go back home to Bay de Verde. Frank gave his friend the information on the burning vessel and asked him to telegraph a message to St. John's as soon as he arrived.

After receiving the message, the government search and rescue people tried contacting the *Seal* but got no response. Perhaps slightly suspicious about the validity of the report, the authorities contacted the man in Bay de Verde wanting to know who had sighted the burning vessel. When they learned that it was Frank Ryan, the lightkeeper on Baccalieu Island, they immediately dispatched the *Eagle* to go to the rescue. When the *Eagle* arrived on the scene several hours later, the *Seal* was a total loss but all the crewmembers were safe on the ice floes.

The master of the *Seal*, Captain Samuel Barbour, realized that had it not been for the keen observance and quick thinking of Frank Ryan, it might have been too late when they were sighted. As a token of his appreciation, Captain Barbour, sent Frank Ryan a berth to go to the seal hunt each spring. Frank never did accept the captain's offer for himself. Instead, he trans-ferred his berth to a friend each year.

The End of the Ryan Era

After ninety-three years of taking care of the Baccalieu lighthouse, the Ryan dynasty ended in 1950. Newfoundland became part of Canada in 1949 and, as new Cana-dians, Jim and Edmund Ryan were quick to recognize new and different employment opportuni-ties in Toronto. Along with their mother, Charlotte, the brothers decided to join their brother John

Courtesy Ryan family

L-R Edmund Ryan, Mrs. Charlotte Ryan, John Ryan.

and sister Mary who had already settled in the Ontario city.

On September 15, 1950 the St. John's *Daily News* wrote a tribute to the Ryan family:

> The Ryans have gone from Baccalieu Island and thereby hangs a tale — a tale of endurance of courage, of faith in God and their fellow man. James, Edmund and their mother left here recently for Toronto where modern apartments will take place of their sea-girt home and where the hue and the cry of men will replace the songs of their feathered friends.
>
> The Ryans were favourably known to mariners and fishermen. Because of their isolation, they loved, not man the less but nature more. The Ryans are gone but the light, the one that James lit ninety-three years ago, will continue to send its rays seaward.

Chapter Twelve

Children of the Lights

Many sons of lighthouse keepers followed in their father's footsteps. Six generations of the Cantwell family kept the Cape Spear light burning for more than 140 years. Five different Campbell families took care of the light on Cape Norman. Ryans were in charge of the Baccalieu light for nearly a hundred years.

There are several reasons for the dynastic system of operating lighthouses. In some cases in the early days, the principal lightkeeper did all the hiring. In the days when work was hard to find, a steady job with fairly good pay was very attractive to most young men. Government officials liked the idea of handing the reins from father to son too. Coping with life on a lonely island or headland jutting out into the Atlantic Ocean was not for the faint of heart. Government officials preferred to hire young men who grew up on lightstations because they knew the lifestyle and they knew the work.

Perhaps the continuity of family members assuming control of lighthouses explains why there has never been a fatality in Newfoundland involving a lightkeeper's child falling over a cliff. Despite living on the tip of some of the highest and steepest headlands in Newfoundland and Labrador, children of lighthouses scaled the rocks with unbelievable ease. "Sure they were like mountain goats," says Betty Strowbridge, who raised two children on St. Jacques Island.

Adapting to their rocky environment from the minute they were able to crawl, children who lived and played on the cliffs of Baccalieu, Belle Isle, Cape Pine and other similar locations seemed to intuitively understand the dangers of their play area early in life. Some women confess they had no alternative but to make a harness for their very young children and tie them to a lead when they were outdoors. One misplaced step meant almost certain death in the rock-infested waters at the bottom of the steep cliffs.

"What else could we do?" one woman questioned. Asking not to be identified for fear of offending today's children's rights activists, she pointed out that taking care of five or six children in addition to a daily workload that had no end left her no choice if she wanted to let her child outside. "It was either we put them in a harness or they never saw the light of day till they were five or six and that was not an option."

Calvin Chant grew up on Ireland's Island on the southwest coast. He says he and his sisters were not allowed out of the house in winter. At only forty feet above sea level, the tiny rocky enclave was almost constantly coated in ice due to freezing spray in winter. With eight children to keep an eye on, Calvin's mother, Lily, couldn't take a chance on letting them outside until spring.

Although there have been no fatalities involving children falling from cliffs, there were plenty of close calls. "There must have been plenty of guardian angels in those days," says Cyril Myrick. Cyril's cousin, Noel Myrick, laughs when he talks about the numerous times his brother Eugene fell down the cliffs on Cape Race. Although Eugene was injured on several occasions, he always managed to survive with only a few broken bones and scrapes and bruises.

Hubert Miles from Fortune remembers the day when he and his colleague Walt Strowbridge discovered Hubert's four-year-old son Keith nonchalantly sitting on the edge of the cliff on St. Jacques Island, his legs dangling over the rocks. A sudden gust of wind or a falling rock could have easily toppled the little fellow from the cliff into the rocky waters nearly a hundred feet below. The boy was the playful type and usually when his father or Walt came close he would run away, daring them to catch him if they could — hide and seek was his favourite game. Hubert and Walt worried that if they approached the boy too quickly, he would forget where he was and start playing his usual game and scurry out to the very end of the cliff.

Careful not to distract him, Walt and Hubert pretended to ignore Keith as Hubert tied a rope around Walt and secured it to a turnbuckle fastened in the rock near the edge of the cliff. Walt slowly rappelled his way down the cliff until he reached Keith who, true to his reputation, thought Walt was coming down to play a game and had no intentions of being rescued. Just as Keith started to scamper away, Walt, hanging unto the rope with one hand, managed to grab the little guy by the shoulder. Luckily he could hold on long enough to convince the child to stop squirming, suggesting they go back up the hill and play a real game that his dad could also join in. Today, Walt Strowbridge remembers that incident as "touch and go, for a while."

Irene Dicks says her brother Michael pushed her halfway down the cliff at Tide's Point when she was about six years old. Quick to point out that they were simply playing and that Michael was not angry, Irene laughs heartily at the incident now but she knows she came close to being seriously injured, if not killed. "We were playing out on the Point and I got into an empty barrel to hide away from the others," she says. Michael soon discovered his sister's hiding place and instead of sneaking up and announcing to the other children that he had found his sister, he decided to push the barrel to give his young sister a little scare. It was Michael who got the biggest fright. Forgetting that the ground was covered in slippery, frozen snow, Michael was horrified to see the barrel sliding toward the steep cliffs of Tide's Point. Luckily the barrel struck some brush on the side of the cliff, breaking its speed, allowing Irene time to scramble out. "If the barrel had gone a few more feet to the right, I might have been killed because the next stop was the bottom of the cliff," Irene says.

Mike Kendall still carries a deep scar on his forehead from a serious fall when he was just five years old. Mike didn't fall over a cliff. His injuries resulted from a fall from the concrete wall of a construction project near the lighthouse.

"Saturday, May 14, 1966, was a fine day," Mike's mother, Melissa Kendell, recalls. The weather had been stormy for nearly a week and the Kendell children were eager to get outdoors after days of confinement in the house. After a full day playing their favourite outdoor games, Mike and his older brother, Gary, finished supper that evening and asked permission to go out for another hour to continue their fun. Feeling sorry for the children after their five-day storm-restricted playtime, Melissa and her husband Wilson reluctantly agreed to let the boys outside to play until dark. Fifteen minutes later Melissa wished she hadn't been so kind. Lightkeeper Howard Sheppard came running up the walkway to the house shouting to Wilson to come quickly because Mike had fallen headfirst onto a concrete floor in a partially constructed building near the lighthouse. Melissa knew from Howard's anxiety that her son was hurt, but she had no idea of the extent of Mike's injuries. After cleaning off the blood to get a look at the wounds, it was soon obvious to Melissa, Wilson and Howard that Mike had severe head injuries and needed immediate medical attention.

Wilson and Howard radioed the nearest Coast Guard station requesting assistance, but they were advised that the nearest helicopter was located in Gander. With just minutes remaining before darkness fell, the chopper wouldn't make it to South Head until daylight. The Kendells were afraid that Mike wouldn't survive until the next morning, so they quickly considered their only option — they had to get Mike off South Head by boat.

Rough seas and a low tide made it impossible to launch the dory from South Head and it would be nearly impossible to get a large boat near enough to the rocks to get Mike onboard. "There's only one man I know who can land a boat here this evening and I hope to God he's home," Wilson said to his wife. The Kendells' luck soon took a turn for the better. Minutes after a phone call from a Coast Guard operator, Albert Sheppard, a fisherman known as a keen hand to manoeuvre a boat, was speeding toward South Head from his home in Lark Harbour, six miles away. Despite rough seas, the fisherman made it to South Head in less than a half an hour. The only place he could attempt to land was in a small cave-like nook, carved out millions of years ago by glaciers, underneath overhanging black rocks. Although he knew the cliffs well, Albert needed to execute precision timing to barely touch shore and leave again within seconds. About forty feet offshore, Albert rode the waves in his powered dory like a cowboy atop a bronco, waiting for just the right moment to make a run for it. Waiting on the shoreline, Wilson stood, holding his son in his arms, while Howard crouched, ready to grab the dory.

For Melissa Kendell, the scene was a nightmare in slow motion. Watching from the lighthouse window, she often wanted to close her eyes and pretend she was dreaming but, desperately praying to see her baby get onboard the boat, she stared motionless, as if in a trance. Once, just moments after the small speedboat nearly disappeared from her view in the trough of two large waves, she saw Albert speeding towards shore. "From the rocks, I saw Howard frantically signalling to Albert to stop because there was a big crashing wave right behind the boat." Fortunately, Albert saw the signal and managed to put the engine in reverse just in time to avoid being bashed against the cliff.

A second attempt to land also failed. Finally, on the third run, all the right factors came together. As if directed by some magical choreographer, Albert surfed a wave and brought the dory close enough for Howard to grab. While Howard steadied the boat for a few seconds, Wilson jumped aboard with Mike in his arms. Wasting no time, Albert quickly reversed the outboard motor while Howard pushed with all his might to get the boat away from the rocks before another oncoming wave threw it against the cliff. They were just in time. Seconds later, a huge wave that would have smashed the speedboat into splinters crashed against the cliffs, filling the nook with hissing white water.

Twenty minutes later, Albert arrived in Lark Harbour where Melissa's brother, Winston Childs, met him at the wharf. Winston, who was home on leave from the Canadian Armed Forces, rushed the injured boy to the Corner Brook Hospital for treatment.

Mike Kendell is lucky to be alive. He arrived at the hospital and underwent surgery in time to lead to a full recovery. Had it not been for the boating skills and courage of Albert Sheppard, he might have died.

Ironically, both Albert Sheppard and Mike Kendell later worked for the Coast Guard. Albert became a lightkeeper while Mike, who

still carries a deep scar on his forehead from the accident, is employee
with Coast Guard, Fisheries and Oceans in St. John's.

Suppose One of Us Gets Sick

Lightkeepers living in remote locations, especially those on islands
constantly worried about medical emergencies during bad weather
What would happen, they wondered, if someone suddenly became
ill and required immediate medical attention to save them from
death?

Fred and Daphne Osbourne didn't worry too much about anything until one week in 1969 when their son became very ill. Fred
Junior, who was less than a year old at the time, was running a
temperature of 104°. There were no plans for a boat or helicopter to
come to the island in the immediate future, so the best Fred and
Daphne could do was contact a doctor at the St. Anthony hospital by
phone. The doctor suggested she rub the child with alcohol to cool
him, but after a couple of days Fred and Daphne realized their son
needed more than a rubdown with a cooling agent. He needed
medical attention and he needed it right away. After encountering
what Fred still considers indifference by the Coast Guard to his
attempt to get the child off the island, he approached the principal
lightkeeper with a simple, but straightforward, message. "If they
don't get a helicopter in for my son right away, they can send the *Sir
Humphrey Gilbert* down and take me, bag and baggage — I don't have
to put up with this bullshit."

They did send the chopper and the boy was taken to hospital in
St. Anthony where he responded favourably to treatment. It was
then that Fred realized it was time to look for a station that was less
remote and more accessible to services in case of family emergencies.
A little while later he was transferred.

It wasn't only lighthouse people who lived on islands that worried about the consequences of medical emergencies. Lighthouses
are usually perched on a headland where, in winter, it's often nearly
impossible to go outside.

"My biggest worry was fire on those days, but I often wondered
about what would happen supposing one of us got sick during bad

weather, especially one of the children," says Faith Sheppard. Fortunately, Faith never had to deal with a fire at any of lighthouses she lived in, but she almost lost her son to illness when she and her husband Max were stationed at Point Amour, Labrador.

On Christmas Eve 1966, two-year-old Max Sheppard Jr. contracted a severe case of red measles. On Boxing Day, the young boy was running an extremely high temperature and became very ill. Faith knew her son needed medical attention, but Point Amour was seized in the grip of a heavy snowstorm. Under normal circumstances, the closest hospital in Long Point, Quebec was a forty-five minute drive away, but that day Faith knew it would take much longer to get there, if they could make it at all. At first she wondered if it might be safer to wait out the storm. She knew that taking her son out in a storm might even worsen his condition. As she waited, the storm intensified while her son kept getting worse and worse. Finally Faith couldn't take it any longer.

Faith knew it would be almost impossible to drive their family car to the hospital in Long Point. The first, and perhaps biggest, challenge was getting from the lighthouse to the Labrador Straits Highway. But as her child grew weaker, she became desperate and decided that she had to do something. Knowing that she and Max couldn't possibly make it on their own, she decided to enlist help.

Bobby Davis, Stewart Hancock, Cecil Davis, Wilfred Davis and Hal Davis from L'Anse Amour answered the call. As the men arrived at the lighthouse armed with snow shovels, their first task was to dig out Max's car from under a huge snow bank. As they shovelled, someone remembered a farm tractor that was stored in the garage. It was only a garden-variety tractor used to carry out odd jobs around the lighthouse, but it was equipped with large tires that had good traction in snow. Maybe they could tow the car out from the snow bank and get thing moving much more quickly, they thought. It turned out to be a good idea. The men hitched a cable from the tractor to the car, and after a few tugs, the car was on the road.

After bundling the baby in warm clothing, Faith took Max Jr. in her arms and got in the front seat of the car as her husband sat behind the wheel, preparing to brave the Labrador storm. The man driving

the tractor went ahead, beating a path and sometimes towing the ca
through the highest snowdrifts until they finally reached the mai
road. Inching their way along, everyone hoped that once the
reached Forteau, the weather would be better. They hoped in vai
In fact, Faith remembers that if there was any change in Forteau,
was for the worse. Wild winds lashed the snow so violently that
was practically impossible to see. "You couldn't see a hand in front o
your face," is the way Faith describes the scene.

Although the weather didn't cooperate, they did get one lucky
break in Forteau. Jim Letto, the snowplough operator, was just
leaving to plough the roads from Forteau west to the Quebec border.
Driving as closely as they dared behind the plough, Max and Faith
continued their journey in relative comfort, albeit not as quickly as
they would have liked. By then, the baby had started convulsing.

Finally, they reached Black Rocks on the Quebec/Labrador border where Dr. Marcoeux from the Long Point hospital and hospital
employee Rene Jones were waiting in a covered snowmobile to meet
them. The storm had heightened to such intensity that someone had
to walk in front of the snowmobile to guide the driver along. What
would normally be a thirty-minute trip took them two and a half
hours.

Luckily they made it just in time. Still convulsing and in critical
condition, two-year-old Max Sheppard would probably have died
that night if they had not made it to the hospital when they did. He
was immediately placed in intensive care where, although it was
"touch and go for a while," Faith says, he finally responded to
treatment. It took a month of hospital care to nurse the young boy to
being well enough to go home to his family.

School Days

Raising small children in relative isolation without other children
around was always a challenge for parents. But one of the most
difficult times for them was when their children became school-aged.
In many cases, the lightkeepers' wives schooled their children
through the elementary grades, but when they reached the age of ten
or eleven, they usually had to leave home to attend school. That was

almost always the case for children of lightkeeping families on small remote islands that were almost always totally isolated in winter. Most lighthouse keepers and their wives were relatively well-educated and insisted that their children receive a good education too. While parents understood the value of educating their children, it was heartbreaking for them to send their young ones away to live in boarding houses on the Newfoundland "mainland" to get that education.

To avoid that trauma, some lighthouse keepers even paid a teacher to come and live with the family at the lighthouse rather then send their children to a different community. Frank Ryan, who kept the light on Baccalieu Island for fifty years, paid a teacher $10 a month to teach his four children. While it doesn't seem like a lot of money these days, $100 a year, in addition to providing free room and board for the teacher, amounted to a sizeable portion of the lightkeepers' salary in the 1930s.

For the Ryan children, it was practically a tutorial system of schooling. "We'd get up in the morning and after breakfast, we'd go into the parlour to attend school — with only the four of us, it was almost like having a teacher all to yourself," says Mary Ryan.

Although less fortunate than the Ryans, most children who had to leave home at a young age to attend school were well cared for in familiar surroundings. Usually they went to live with relatives in the former hometown of one of their parents. Not only was it less traumatic for the children, it was also comforting for the parents knowing their children were safe and secure with family.

While most of the children suffered the usual anxieties of being away from their parents and family at first, a lot of them eventually grew to feel that they had two homes.

Epilogue

The End of an Era

The days of kerosene lights and steam-operated fog alarms have long gone. So have the days when ship's captains sent sailors to the bow to watch for a sign of land through dense fog. Electronic gadgetry on vessels of all sizes tells mariners their precise location anywhere in the world. Radar and other equipment allow captains to see through the thickest fog as if it were a sunny day in July. Lights and fog alarms are now run by computerized gizmos that can be operated by a technician hundreds of miles away from the lighthouse.

Those technological advances have replaced the need for traditional lighthouse keeping. Whether all lights should be run by remote control is a matter of intense public debate in some circles. Many people argue that machines and electronic equipment will never provide the same level of surveillance that a lightkeeper does. They point out that as long as there are waters frequented by small commercial and recreational boats, there will always be a need for staffed lighthouses in case of accidents.

While that debate continues, there is no argument over the tremendous service and contributions that lighthouse keepers have made to Newfoundland and Labrador society. Theirs was a life of survival against incredible odds while, at the same time, their primary concern was caring for others. Most lighthouse keepers and their families are quiet and unassuming, never considering their sacrifices as anything more than just doing their job.

As guardians of the rugged coastlines of Newfoundland and

Labrador, the thousands of men and women who dedicated the
every moment to providing safety to ships at sea should never k
forgotten.

Graveyard at Cape Norman Lighthouse. The more than thirty people buried in
the graveyard are Campbells. Note the lighthouse at the top of the hill.

Courtesy Canadian Coast Guard, Fisheries and Oceans

St. Mike's Head light, 1920. Lamp was lit at ground level and then hoisted to the top of the wooden frame.

Great Dernier light tower in 1900 — supported by wooden shores to keep from blowing into the ocean. Obviously, not all lighthouses were majestic beacons and towers.

Lighthouse at Rose Blanche — one of few in the world constructed of granite rock. The all-in-one light and residence has been restored to near its original characteristics, and is now a major tourist attraction.

Courtesy Doug Peet

Hoisting winter supplies from a small boat — typical scene on islands where light-houses were located.

Former lighthouse residence, St. Anthony (Fishing Point) — now a restaurant.

Former Lighthouse residence, Cape Ray — now a craft shop.